The History of
Castlemorton's Commons,
Coombe Green Common and
Marsh Green Common

by
David Smallwood

GSP

The History of Castlemorton's Commons, Coombe Green Common,
and Marsh Green Common

David Smallwood

Published by Greyhound Self-Publishing 2022
Malvern, Worcestershire, United Kingdom.

Printed and bound by Aspect Design
89 Newtown Road, Malvern, Worcs. WR14 1PD United Kingdom
Tel: 01684 561567
E-mail: allan@aspect-design.net
Website: www.aspect-design.net

Cover Design Copyright © 2022
Cover Photograph: Reverend Douglas Tassell looking out over
his garden gate in about 1972,
courtesy of Jean Pennant, his daughter

ISBN: 978-1-909219-94-6

CONTENTS

"Moved by J Weaver, seconded by M Fellows, that the Clerk and Mr Price visit Malvern Library and look up the history of Castlemorton Common and see what information they can get on the matter."

Castlemorton Parish Council minutes, 24 April 1925

INTRODUCTION

Much has been written about the history of Malvern Chase and its villages, but little specifically about Castlemorton Common and the other common land in the area. This publication seeks to fill that gap and I thank the many people who have helped in the production of this publication.

The management of the common has been a matter of much local concern for decades and it is hoped that this history will give some clarity as to how things were and how they came to be as they are now. In the process, a few myths may even be dispelled!

All common land has an owner. You might think that it belongs to everyone, but that is not so, although we all have certain rights to access and use common land. The legal position was clarified by the Commons Registration Act of 1965, which required the ownership of all common land to be registered with local authorities, in our case with Worcestershire County Council. A definitive map of all common land in the County can be inspected there. However, it is much easier to Google 'magic defra' which will take you to **magic.defra.gov.uk/MagicMap.aspx**. Select

'Access' and then 'Registered Common Land' and zoom in see a detailed map of all common land in the local area.

This history covers Castlemorton/Hollybed Common (which embraces Golden Valley), and Shady Bank Common – all owned by Malvern Hills Trust. It also covers Coombe Green Common (which adjoins Hollybed Common) and is privately owned by the Dawes family of Birtsmorton Court; and Marsh Green Common (also known as Lower Common) which is owned by the Smith family of Hillend Court.

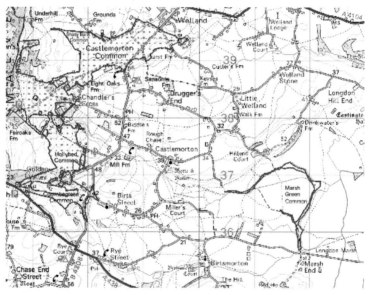

Common Land is shown in green. (Magic Maps)

Areas

Castlemorton/Hollybed	648 acres
Shady Bank Common	29 acres
Coombe Green Common	49 acres
Marsh Green Common	34 acres

Llama trekking.

Kite flying.

You Tube

There are videos of the area on YouTube. Go to YouTube first and then search for:

Gullet Quarry Castlemorton

Castlemorton Common to Gullet Quarry

Mavic2Pro Asteroid Effect Castlemorton

Films

In 1927 a silent film, "The King's Highway", was made in Castlemorton. Copies are not available. You can view it by appointment at the British Film Archive - look out for the washing hanging on the line!

In 2012 part of a film about World War II, "Our Father", was filmed on Castlemorton Common.

Notes

I have referred to Malvern Hills Conservators (the Conservators) on matters prior to 2017, and Malvern Hills Trust (the Trust) after that date. In 2017, with the approval of The Charities Commission, they changed their working title to Malvern Hills Trust, although their legal name is still Malvern Hills Conservators.

An older name for the area of Castlemorton Common towards Gloucester Road was Lower Common and should not be confused with Marsh Green Common.

Chapter 1

WILLIAM THE CONQUEROR TO
KING CHARLES I (1632)

It is not known when the Church first acquired ownership of Castlemorton Common and surrounding lands. It would have been given them by a royal charter. The idea that land could belong to an individual or body such as the Church, and could be sold to anybody else, was new to England in the late 600s and was called Bookland. This distinguished it from the only previous type of land ownership, Folkland. Folkland referred to land held by a single person as the representative of a kinship group. Land could be permanently transferred outside of the kinship group, but only with the agreement of the king, advised by his noblemen. Failing that, land could be transferred only within the kinship group, for example through inheritance.

Michael Wood, in his book "Domesday – A search for the Roots of England", explains that when the Anglo Saxons converted to Christianity in the 650s they "were anxious to make the most of the power offered to them by the Church. To do so, they had to endow the Church with land from the estates they had appropriated as conquerors of this former province of the Roman world." Perhaps this is how Castlemorton Common came into church ownership.

William the Conqueror invaded England in 1066 and by the 1080s he had designated certain regions as Royal Forests. The term Forest in the ordinary modern understanding refers to an area of wooded land; however, the original medieval sense was closer to the modern idea of a "preserve" – i.e. land legally set aside for specific purposes such as royal hunting - with less emphasis on its composition. If the monarch granted the hunting rights to one of his subjects, then it was known as a Chase. One such area was Malvern Chase and this included Castlemorton Common.

Royal Forests usually included large areas of heath, grassland and wetland - anywhere that supported deer and other game. In addition, when an area was initially designated forest, any villages, towns and fields that lay within it were also subject to forest law. This could foster resentment as the local inhabitants were then restricted in the use of land they had previously relied upon for their livelihoods; however, common rights were not extinguished, but merely curtailed. They were not allowed to fence their properties to protect their crops and if the deer trampled on them or ate them they could only ask the forest officials to drive them off.

Edward I (1239-1307) granted Malvern Chase as royal property to Gilbert de Clare, Earl of Gloucester, and it was henceforth called a Chase. This right was inherited through the family until it reached George, Duke of Clarence, who left one son. This son and heir was beheaded in the Tower on pretence of conspiracy in 1478. The King then seized upon all the family's possessions, including the land in Castlemorton.

In her book "The Forest and Chase of Malvern", Pamela Hurle explains that by the 1570s Forest Law had been ignored for at least a generation and probably much longer. A document of 1581 set out orders by fifteen substantial landowners to end abuses and preserve the Chase. These included orders to protect young trees, to stop the use of Chase wood for the commercial purposes of baking, brewing and pottery, and to protect trees which were significant landmarks.

By 1630, Charles I was desperate for money to fight a

war with Spain and Parliament would not give it to him. He had had the Chase valued and mapped in 1628 (7000 acres in Worcestershire, 600 in Herefordshire and 100 in Gloucestershire). A nineteenth century colour painting of the map is held by The Society of Antiquaries and is reproduced in Pamela Hurle's book. It shows Castlemorton Common as belonging to the Dean & Chapter of Westminster (who had 1563 acres in Castlemorton) and to have "no timber but much underwood".

The King decided to give up his rights to two thirds of the chase, and keep one third of the land for himself which he could then sell to raise money. This one third is known as The King's Third.

A decree was issued in 1632 for the "disafforestation of the Chace of Malvern, that is of freeing the lands within the bounds, limits, and jurisdictions thereof, and from the game of deer there and the forest laws." By this decree one-third part only was to be severed and divided by commissioners, but the other two parts "shall remain and continue unto and amongst the commoners, and be held by them according to their several rights and interests, discharged and freed from his Majesty's game of deer there, and of and from the forest laws, and the liberties and franchises of Forest and Chace, in such sort as by the said decree it doth and may appear."

Besides the tenants and commoners, several powerful landowners, with rights or claims upon the Chace, opposed the execution of this decree.

To end the dispute an Order in Council was made in 1632, to explain the former decree, and for "the settlement of the differences" that had disturbed the country. By this it is declared that the third part to be enclosed should not be the best selected, but "indifferently taken, bad and good," and that "the other two parts shall be left open and free for the freeholders and tenants and commons, to take their common of pasture and common of estovers (*the right to collect wood*) therein" with the restriction that no enclosure shall he made, or woods or trees felled within the two reserved third parts.

The 1628 map shows modern roads: Hollybed Street, Church Road (called Peiry Lane - Perry Lane after pear cider) - and The Hollow (now Green Lane leading from Gloucester Road, past Rose Cottage to Keyses Farm).

The area west and south of Millpond at Golden Valley, including the properties north of the A438 at Hollybush, is marked as an Assart belong to the Dean & Chapter of Westminster. This means that the King had already relinquished his rights there and the ground had been cleared for cultivation. Here 80 acres had been granted by lease to John Renford. A second Assart marked on the map, north of Hancocks Lane would also have been part of Castlemorton Common. It is marked as "Assart clayes by Mr Russell" - John Russell of Little Malvern - whose family married the Beringtons who became owners of Little Malvern Court. In 1949 a sale of Berington properties owned by Little Malvern Court included Gate Cottage, partly in the parish of Castlemorton and bordering the common.

An area adjoining what is the now Castlemorton common, between Dales Hall and the common on the east, must originally have also been common land. We know this because it was part of the land which the king kept for himself – the King's Third. It is outlined in red on the map and today is owned by Tim Cameron of Dales Hall, David Weaver of Mount Pleasant and Colin Weaver of Kingswear. The area inside it bounded by the green line is owned by Malvern Hills Trust and includes two fields recently purchased from the Clutterbuck family.

The area to the south, now largely the Fairoaks Estate, was also originally part of the common. The small area at the southern end shows an additional area that might also have been part of the King's Third.

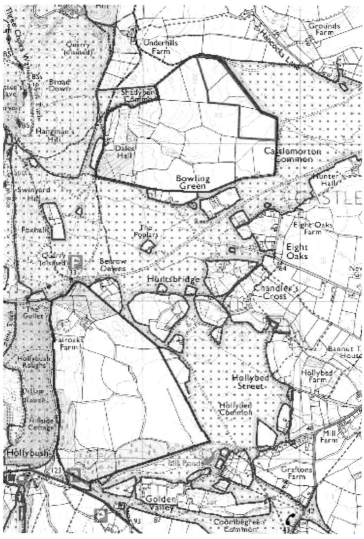

The red boundary shows two areas of the King's Third which would originally have been part of the common.

Chapter 2

UNDER THE DEAN AND CHAPTER OF WESTMINSTER [4] 1632-1836

Enclosure

During the 1700s and 1800s, parts of common land in England were enclosed (taken into private ownership), sometimes by locals encroaching onto small areas and sometimes by Enclosure Acts. Properties on the commons today, surrounded by common land, would originally have been part of the common itself and each has its own story about how it became enclosed.

In 1814, a Bill was prepared when the Lords of other Chase parishes proposed to enclose the common land. "It would be of great Benefit and Advantage to the several persons entitled and interested in same if the said Rights of Common were extinguished …. and the lands divided and inclosed to those with an interest in the same."

However, Lord Somers of Eastnor addressed the proprietors and freeholders on Malvern Chase saying he had given up all attempts to enclose it as it was impossible to reconcile so many conflicting interests. Many other local parishes did have their common land enclosed and their fate is described by Cora Weaver in her MA Thesis "Forest Law", a copy of which is in Malvern Library under Local Studies Reference Books.

In 1827, it seems that local people were having to deal with encroachment themselves. A document records 18 residents [1] agreeing to bear an equal share of the solicitor's costs in dealing with certain encroachments and trespassers.

15

Relationships between the residents of the common and the Dean & Chapter of Westminster were often strained as is shown the case between the Dean and Chapter of Westminster and Berington Esq in 1835. An action of ejectment was brought by the ecclesiastical body to recover three pieces of land in the possession of the defendant, and which they claimed as encroachments upon The Waste of the Manor of Castlemorton, of which they were Lords. There would probably be no dispute as to the fact of their having been originally enclosed from the waste, but the defendant claimed to be entitled to them as Lord of the Manor of Little Malvern. After the first witness was called, the learned Judge suggested that the only question in dispute was the exact line of boundary, which could not be determined in the present action, whatever the decision might be, it would be much more to the interests of both parties to agree to refer that question to some gentleman at the bar, who would examine the spot and set out such boundary line, by metes and bounds, and prevent any disputes arising upon the subject in future. After some discussion it was agreed to refer the question of boundary to Mr. Alexander, each party paying their own costs of the action, and the costs of the reference to be divided.

Another action in 1836 was between the Dean and Chapter of Westminster and Henry Higgins of The Myttons. It was alleged that a man in the pay of the Dean and Chapter was selling the freehold of common land to cottagers. Subsequently, the Dean & Chapter sought to repossess the land and instead of returning it to the waste as common land, they rented it back to the cottager, who could not afford the legal costs of contesting the matter. [2]

Crime

Stealing animals grazing on the common was regarded as a very serious offence, as shown by two of the following cases.

In 1818, R. Harris was sentenced to death for stealing a horse from Castlemorton Common.

In 1831, at the Warwick Assizes, Thomas Morris was charged with stealing a mare, belonging to Thomas Coulston. On the 28th of June, Coulston had a brown mare, which he turned out on Castlemorton Common. He missed her the next day, but afterwards, in consequence of information he had received, he went to Nuneaton and found her in the possession of John Baraclough who kept the Old Crown Inn, with whom the prisoner had swapped her for another horse. The prisoner was seen by several persons with the mare in her possession. Morris was sentenced to death.

In 1832, at Worcester Assizes, Josiah Bullock, 20, was charged with stealing a pony (the property of John Brookes) from Castlemorton Common on the 28th of June. Mr. Pumfrey, farmer at Kinlet, Shropshire, bought the pony from two men he met on the road. He could not swear the prisoner was one of them. His servant, William Davis, proved that he was, but that the other received the money. Hannah Morris (Bullock's sister) swore that Bullock was at her house when the pony was stolen. Bullock was acquitted.

The Tithe Maps

Tithe maps were produced for Birtsmorton in 1837 and Castlemorton in 1839. They are very detailed and show who owned and who occupied every piece of land in the Parish, including the common and the properties on and around it. [3]

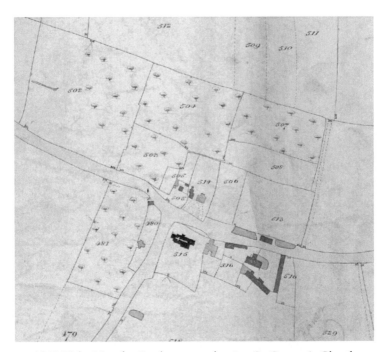

*1839 Tithe Map for Castlemorton, showing St Gregory's Church.
(No 515)*

Chapter 3

UNDER THE CHURCH COMMISSIONERS
1837-1927

In 1836, the ownership of Castlemorton common was transferred to the Ecclesiastical Commissioners and in 1948 to the Church Commissioners.

By 1845, about 400 acres of the remaining Saxon common fields and hay meadows on the east of Gloucester Road had been enclosed and divided amongst the farms and freeholders. [5] Ten years later a similar proposal came forward for Castlemorton Common. [6]

A handwritten notice dated 25th July 1855 [7] announced that "Notice is hereby given that a meeting will be holden in the Vestry room of this Parish on Friday the third day of August next at ten o'clock in the forenoon to consider the expediency of inclosing the commonable and waste lands within this Parish and if the same should then be decided upon to adopt and carry such resolutions as may then be thought most advisable for affecting the purposes aforesaid and for other general purposes."

Following a mass meeting at The Plume of Feathers, there was such opposition that the proposal to inclose the common was abandoned.

In 1875 we learn from a newspaper account that the police had the power to remove diseased animals from the Common. William Pinson, of Upton upon Severn, was summoned for having sheep affected with scab, without reporting the same to the police. Richard Potts, sergeant of police at Welland, stated that the defendant came to his house and informed him his sheep were affected with scab and that he had removed them from Castlemorton Common. The witness examined them and found that they must have been suffering from scab for some time before the defendant reported them. The defendant was fined 2s. 6d. and costs, or in default 14 days. Charles H. Lawrence, of Redmarley D'Abitot, was charged with a similar offence on Castlemorton Common. PC Griffin stated that he examined sheep belonging to the defendant, and found them affected with scab. Defendant said he did not know they were so affected. He was fined 2s 6d. and costs, in default 11 days.

On 21 September 1895. Prudence Smith, a travelling gipsy, was charged by Elias Walters with damaging the turf on Castlemorton Common by cutting holes in it. Elias Walters said he saw the defendant and a man on the common with a fire. He told them they could not stay there, but they remained in spite of his warning. This summons was taken out on the authority of the Ecclesiastical Commissioners. The Bench fined the defendant 1s. damages and remitted the costs.

In 1901, it still seems that local people were having to take control of misuse of the common, as W Whittle and friends instructed Solicitors to prosecute Mr F S Gilbert for exercising horses on the common. The case is interesting because the Solicitors had to point out that there was no such thing as a common right to exercise horses and that only the High Court had any jurisdiction in this matter, not the County Court. [8]

In 1906 [9] there was an enquiry by the County Council. Its purpose was to determine who were the claimants to common rights, the nature of their claims, and then as to what the rights of common were. This would enable the County Council to determine what rules should be made as to the turning out of animals. The common should be used by the person with the rights to do so and the purpose of the enquiry was for determining who those persons were. Mr Cazalet, Chairman of the Parish Council and owner of The Bannut Tree and other farms, said the custom was for every resident of the Parish to turn out whatever cattle he liked. This applied equally to new houses as well as houses built in time immemorial. Silas Weaver explained that all the inhabitants had the unrestricted right to turn out cattle on the common and that right had never been challenged. However, custom was only to turn out as much stock in the summer as they could keep on their own land in the winter. Mr Foster, a freeholder, said these rights had caused a rise in house prices in recent years. Silas Weaver added that it had always been the custom for owners of freehold to crop the trees near his land for stakes and poles. Young men were growing up in the Parish and population was increasing – the good ones acquired a few sheep, often starting with a lamb when they were 13 or 14, and turned them out on the common and from these small beginnings many had become substantial farmers. If the rights were interfered with it would mean throwing the common into the hands of large farmers and the grass was not good enough for their class of cattle.

By 1908, the County Council had conducted their enquiry and their General Purposes Committee voted in favour of making regulations for taking control of Castlemorton Common. They would seek a lease from the Ecclesiastical Commissioners for 30 years for not more than £10 a year.

They would not seek to interfere with commoners rights. At this time, there was nothing to stop anyone doing what they pleased on the common and the County Council wished to "render this large tract of waste liable to the general bye-laws which had been passed as regarded open spaces in other parts of the country. That was in pursuance of the policy adopted by the Council for preserving for the good of the country those open spaces and to prevent depredations". The lease they sought was the lease to manorial rights. The only regulations to be made under the lease were to prohibit gaming, hawking, lighting fires, placing rubbish, causing damage, erecting booths or placing caravans, using firearms, taking game, rabbits or birds, removing sand, turf, fern, and gorse.

In 1909, a meeting was called in the Parish Hall to discuss the matter of common land and smallholdings. This suggests that there had been a miscommunication between the Parish and the County; the Parish believing that commoners rights were in jeopardy and the County not wishing to interfere with them at all. In a letter of 13 August 1909, from the Commons and Footpaths Preservation Society to Robert Weaver of Bricklands, he was advised that only the Board of Agriculture could decide on commoners rights and that rights belonged to properties, not individuals. Claims to unlimited rights would not be upheld – there had to be some limit. This advice was formalised over 50 years later in the in the Commons Registration Act of 1965.

In 1910, at a Worcestershire County Council meeting, Mr W. S. Lane successfully moved that the Council rescind the resolution directing that a lease be taken from the Ecclesiastical Commissioners.

PARISH OF CASTLEMORTON

Notice of Parish Meeting.

COMMON LANDS AND THE SMALL HOLDINGS ACT, 1907

A MEETING

will be held in the **PARISH HALL, on Wednes-
day, August 25th, 1909,** at 8 o'clock p.m., for the
purpose of considering the proposed action of the
Worcestershire County Council with regard to the
Common Lands of the Parish, and also to suggest a
mode of procedure to those persons who are desirous
of obtaining land in accordance with the above Act who
have not as yet been provided with the same.

ALL PERSONS INTERESTED ARE REQUESTED TO ATTEND.

(Signed)

S. J. WEAVER,

CASTLEMORTON, *Chairman of Parish Council.*

August 13th 1909 *"News." Upton-on-Severn.*

Parish Council poster, 13 August 1909.

While the County Council were concerned that "their"
smallholders would enjoy grazing rights, the Parish Council
and the local community clearly rejected what they regarded
as unwarranted external bureaucratic interference in local
affairs.

The Small Holdings and Allotments Act 1907 empowered

23

County Councils to "provide small holdings for persons who desire to buy or lease and will themselves cultivate the holdings". If sufficient demand for smallholdings was established, Councils could be obliged to implement schemes to acquire and provide the land required. The earlier Smallholdings Act of 1892 merely permitted Councils to acquire land for sub division and sale as smallholdings and had little impact.

By early 1909 Worcestershire County Council had received applications in respect of some 8,600 acres from 862 aspiring smallholders. In the parish of Castlemorton, 55 applicants sought, in aggregate, more than 700 acres of smallholdings. The County Council struggled to meet this demand, initially acquiring only 23 acres, let to four smallholders.

In contrast, the Parish Council [10] had established an exemplary record in providing smallholdings and allotments [11], assuming the role previously fulfilled by the overseers and churchwardens of the parish.

To quote from an address in 1909 by the Chairman of the National Allotments and Small Holdings Association: "The Castle Morton Parish Council, near Malvern, under the chairmanship of Mr. Weaver, furnishes a convincing proof of the value and gain of Small Holdings where the occupiers have not the advantage of market gardening and the growth of special crops of fruit and vegetables. The Parish Council hires about 220 acres (from the Somers family) re-let in about 70 tenancies, rents from 10s. to 30s. per acre, in lots of from half-an-acre to five acres. Having considerable common rights here, the occupiers winter the sheep, etc., on their small meadows and grow roots and straw crops for winter fodder on the tillage for cattle, colts, etc., also corn for their own consumption. The rents have always been punctually paid, with small exceptions. A few grow vegetables, etc., for Malvern market."

The minutes of the Parish Council from 1909-1927, and later, record the meticulous care being exercised over the proper cultivation by the individual tenants of these allotments. Where allotments were neglected or badly used, the Parish Council was quick to act.

In 1924 there is a report of pilfering by non-residents - gypsies and van dwellers making a prolonged sojourn on the common and indulging in violent back-chat when remonstrances were addressed to them. Mr R Weaver made an urgent appeal to the whole of the parish in support of the discouragement of gipsy encampments on the common. Not only were they a nuisance, but they were disruptive and a source of danger to adjoining properties by lighting fires etc. He had experienced great trouble in this direction.

Chapter 4

UNDER CASTLEMORTON PARISH COUNCIL
1927-1965

In 1926, Castlemorton Parish Council resolved to call a special parish meeting to formulate a scheme whereby the management of the common should be carried out by Parish Council. It was decided to ask the Ecclesiastical Commissioners if they would be willing to give their consent to the Parish Council seeking powers for the regulation of the common. It is doubtful if this would have been legal, as the 1899 Commons Act [12] only gave the power to draw up schemes of regulation to District Councils.

The outcome was that in 1927 Upton upon Severn Rural District Council drew up a scheme of management for the Common, with bye-laws [13] and then delegated responsibility for implementing it to Castlemorton Parish Council, as they represented those who had rights over the common.

In 1928, Castlemorton Parish Council passed a motion for a 6d rate in order to pay the expenses of Upton Rural District Council in carrying out the scheme.

Notice Boards displaying the bye-laws were erected at Shady Bank, Fairoaks near the Gullet, Hollybush Church, Lydiatts, Joyfields, the end of Lower Common by Welland and on Marsh Green Common near Tewkesbury Road.

The bye-laws gave no specific powers for dealing with gypsies. In 1928, the Parish Council received eleven separate complaints about "the intolerable nuisance caused by the utter lack of sanitary arrangements and consequent indecency of about 80 to 100 gypsies now encamped in five camps on Castlemorton Common". These complaints were forwarded to the Sanitary Inspector of the Rural District Council.

In 1929, the Parish Council decided that no holiday camps should be allowed on the common. During the holiday season, in 1933, Mr Hardman, Parish Councillor, moved a camp of holiday makers near Broomy Hill and a camp of gypsies.

In 1933, the Parish Council arranged with the Police to take action on motorists who trespassed on the common, under the Road Traffic Act.

Drainage

In 1934, a drainage scheme for the common was proposed by the County Land Agent. Mr R D Fellows, Vice Chairman of the Parish Council, said that the drainage was in good order 40 years ago and was now silted up and was causing surface water to marsh the common land. The County Council were prepared to pay 85% of the wages and 50% of the cost of tools, providing work for local unemployed men clearing watercourses and drainage ditches. The idea of scheme of drainage was adopted and a survey agreed to.

The Parish Council accepted the scheme with the proviso that the County Council would not in future seek to obtain control of the common on the basis that they had paid to improve it and that the Parish Council would decide what work was to be done. The County Council wrote that they had no intention of seeking any general control and money was given on the same terms as it would be to any other landowner. The Parish Council presumably still had concerns of losing control and rejected the scheme.

Springs

In 1928 the Parish Council noted there was no bye-law dealing direct with the protection of the water supply of the common lands. Water was important for the needs of the growing population of the parish and the animals depastured on the common. They agreed to write to Upton Rural District Council asking for a bye-law for the protection and preservation of the springs, streams, watercourses and the supply of water generally on the common lands.

The District Council replied that they have no power to issue such a bye-law. However, encroachments were illegal and covered by the existing bye-laws. In their opinion the enclosing of a spring in a brick or concrete chamber and the laying of a pipe into the chamber was an encroachment under Section 4 of the Scheme, and the enclosing of a spring in a brick or concrete chamber simply to prevent pollution and with provision that the whole of the water not used by person in ordinary way by persons having undoubted right of use is allowed to escape to the usual channel was also an encroachment.

A test case arose in 1931 when Right Hon J W Wilson [14] of Foxhall [15] installed a new pipe between a spring and his property. He claimed that his property had been supplied with water through a defective old road drain from a spring open to pollution, which he had modernised and that the Ministry of Health would have condemned the old supply and approved the new arrangement. The Parish Council felt his letter evaded the point that the spring was never used by former occupiers of Foxhall for drinking purposes and before reaching his property formerly ran through and supplied a drinking pool for animals on the common and for horses and any vehicular traffic along the road adjacent to the pool. Therefore his action was an encroachment. They asked him to remove the pipe, but he wrote that he now had a Wayleave from the Ecclesiastical Commissioners giving permission for his new pipe. The Ecclesiastical Commissioners agreed not to grant further easements for water pipes without consultation with the Parish Council.

Managing Commoners Rights

At this time, commoners rights had not been formalised and operated on custom and practice. The Parish Council sought to manage these as they felt necessary.

They were concerned about the excessive cropping of trees of the common and the importance of shade for animals in the hot season and shelter especially for newly shorn sheep during heavy rain. They recommended that trees be cropped once every 10 years, in rotation, between 1 November and 1 April.

Parish Council minutes detail the allocation of three trees per property in Hancocks Lane, so that neighbours did not crop trees outside other people's houses.

Problems with people and riding schools galloping horses on the common in the wet season and with people setting rabbit wires or traps are also recorded in the Parish Council minutes.

In 1929, Joseph Bunn of Hunters Hall Farm, was reminded not to cut fern and gorse and then sell it, but only to make manure for his own use. A complaint was made by Mrs Carey [16] that cars were parking on the common in front of her house creating a nuisance.

In 1931, the Parish Council passed a motion that the old

rules of the common that pigs shall not be turned out to the common during the lambing season, and not at all without proper nose rings, shall be enforced.

In 1946, the Church Commissioners leased the sporting rights on the common from January 1946 to February 1947 to Flight Lieutenant F C Brown of the Wells Road.

In 1959, 0.262 acres were enclosed from the common to extend Hollybush Churchyard.

Management Scheme updated

In 1951, Upton Rural District Council wrote to all parishes saying "The Council have for some time been concerned about the apparent neglect of commons in their area and it has been decided that if Parishes were made aware of the necessity to improve their commons and bring their Regulation Schemes up to date, this would probably off-set the compulsory acquisition, at some future date, by the Ministry of Agriculture". A date for a meeting was proposed, but nothing more is recorded.

In 1956, Upton Rural District Council decided to update its delegated authority arrangement with the Parish Council. The Parish Council was required to account for any income from the commons, to obtain approval for any expenditure, and receive applications for grants towards expenditure.

In 1961, Upton Rural District Council sought to amend and supplement their 1927 Scheme (the Bye-Laws). Discussions with the Parish Council dragged on. Shady Bank Common was taken out of the discussions in 1962 because it had been purchased by Malvern Hills Conservators and the Ministry of Agriculture Fisheries and Food approved that the Conservator's Bye-Laws should apply there. The biggest bone of contention was Clause 24, a proposal that no horse, cattle, sheep, pig, goat or other animal should be put out to graze on the common in January or February or any other time prohibited by an order. This was withdrawn.

In 1964 the Conservators purchased Castlemorton Common off the Church Commissioners and Upton Rural District Council relinquished their interest.

Protecting the common

In 1955, a Site of Special Scientific Interest (SSSI) of 392 acres was established over all the common west of Gloucester Road, as far as the eastern side of The Bowling Green. This offered protection to the plants and wildlife benefiting from the grassland, described as the "grassland communities".[17] The common was much clearer of brambles than it is today, because breeds of sheep such as Radnor Cross were grazed and would eat almost anything.

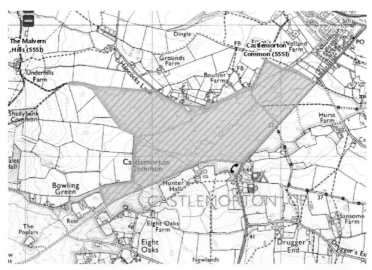

The area of the SSSI. (Magic Maps)

A snapshot of life in Castlemorton in 1956

The Vicar of Castlemorton looks round the Parish that progress passed by and says – "Oh, for the comforts of the jungle". During his four years as a missionary in wildest Tanganyika the Reverend Leslie Budge often dreamed of a return to England and the comforts of civilisation. Now, after four years as vicar of the little Worcestershire village of Castlemorton, he often longs for the modern amenities he left behind in the African jungle. There he could have a good home, with running water and electricity, proper sanitation and on-the-spot medical attention, efficient transport services and recreational facilities. For most of the people of Castlemorton, however, those amenities are no nearer than they were last century, when scores of smallholdings sprang up along the foothills of the Malverns. "Time seems to have stood still here ever since," says the vicar. "For miles around they call this the Forgotten Village, and it could not be more overlooked by the authorities if it had been buried in the African bush. "I have often wondered what one of the natives I taught out in Tanganyika would think if he came to visit me here. The first thing he would notice would be that no children are to be seen playing in the village lanes. There are very few kiddies here, because young married couples are all moving away," explained the vicar. "Why? Because Castlemorton has no Council houses. A plan to build some, after delays totalling 35 years, has been held up again because there is no electricity in that part of the village. Overhead power cables have reached the other end of Castlemorton, but have been stopped there because the Worcestershire Planning Department has ordered that no poles must be erected in this stretch of country."

"This means no piped water supply, for electricity is needed for the pumps," complained farmer Len Bunn, who has been on the Parish Council since 1921. "That means no TT milk from our cattle, although we have everything else to make our herds the best in the country." Mrs. Elsie Lee is fortunate: she lives in a cottage which was linked up with electricity last winter and she is near one of the village's two shops. Her main concern is that there is still no proper sewerage throughout the district. As a mother, she also feels strongly that there is no doctor in Castlemorton and no chemist to make up prescriptions when doctors from Upton upon Severn visit the sick. "It is like living in a lost land," she said. Teenagers

1965, 22 November. Left hand side of road up to Gullet Quarry just before reaching Bowling Green House. This area is very popular for picnicing and children playing games. Result of feeding cattle — loose hay trampled into tracks; heaps of cattle manure all over the area; Commoners occupying land adjoining this area must find great difficulty getting in to their fields.

look outside the village for their work and entertainment, although transport is difficult. When 17-year-old Shirley Clutterbuck set off for a Saturday night dance at Malvern, it meant walking more than a mile to the nearest bus route, with an eight mile taxi trip the only way of getting back home afterwards. Publican John Joseph pointed out that the village has a bus stop, complete with a large timetable board, but no bus has ever been known to go near it. In addition, there is a cricket pitch but no cricket team, no street lamps and no policeman. "Personally, I have no complaints, for the quaint charm of the place attracts hundreds of visitors," said Mr. Joseph. American tourists are always very interested in the name of the village only to be disappointed by the news that Castlemorton, true to tradition, has no castle. [18]

Chapter 5

COMMONERS RIGHTS AND THE REGISTRATION OF COMMON LAND, 1965

In 1955 the Government, realising they knew very little about the scope of common land and commoners rights, appointed The Royal Commission on Public Land (1955-1958) to address four questions:

Who are the commoners?
What are their rights?
Who owns each piece of common land, and where is this in dispute?
What happens with common land that has no commoners and no commoners rights?

They recommended that County Councils should set up registers of Common Land, their owners and the Commoner's Rights, with Commons Commissioners appointed to resolve any disputes. This was brought to fruition by the Commons Registration Act in 1965.

Worcestershire had 4819 acres of common land (1.08% of the County), including 1,310 acres on the Malvern Hills and 812 acres in Castlemorton and Birtsmorton. In England and Wales overall, 2.45% of land was common land.

Commoners Rights

The 1965 Commons Registration Act required all commoners rights [19] [20] to be registered. With grazing rights, the number of animals had to be specified – before 1964 the number of animals that could be grazed depended on the capacity of the common land to feed them. Many properties some distance from the common used to have grazing rights. [21]

Commoners rights are protected for ever. They belong to the property, regardless of who owns it and when a property changes hands it is the responsibility of the new owner to advise Worcestershire County Council so that the register (which is handwritten) can be amended. By appointment, any member of the public can inspect the register and the map of common land.

Claims were made from Castlemorton as shown below, far more than the common could support:

Sheep 10023
Poultry 2397
Cattle 1572
Geese 731
Horses 212
Ducks 52
Sows 295
Donkeys 22
Goats 54
Mules 4

As well the numbers of persons claiming other rights:

Estovers 77
Pescary 70
Pannage 50
Turbary 15

A Mr C A Settle QC was appointed to resolve the claims and he quickly realised the impossibility of the task and handed it over to Castlemorton Commoners Association under the chairmanship of Roger Jakeman.

It was proposed that holdings had to be at least half an acre and should adjoin the common. The allocation was 7 sheep per acre for holdings of between ½ acre and 15 acres, 5 per acre if 15-25 acres, and 3 per acre for holdings over 25 acres. **(22)** Five sheep were to be equivalent to one cow, one horse of pony or one donkey, which may be grazed as an alternative.

The scheme was accepted in 1976. **(23)**

The register has 210 entries, some being deleted, voided or replaced with other entries, leaving 139 valid entries. The total number of sheep and cattle permitted to graze on the common through the registration process is 4421 and 1512 respectively, with other livestock accounting for a further 2840 units. (139 horses, 160 sows, 487 geese, 1995 poultry, 41 goats, 4 donkeys and 14 mules). In addition, the offspring of animals is often allowed, but the numbers are not specified. **(24)**

By 2006 there were only 7 active graziers and in 2019 only about 300 sheep and 70 cattle were being grazed. In 2018, the figures were 450 sheep and 70 cattle, which were regarded as sufficient. Today there are only 6 active commoners: Matt Gardner (Graftons Farm and using Dales Hall's rights), Roy Shail, Dermot Weaver, Barbara Wilkes and Chris Ball (from Welland, using Marlbrook Farm rights). Grazing from Hunters Hall, the largest grazier on the common, came to an end shortly after the death of Ron Bunn in 2006. **(25)**

Common Land

Additionally, the 1965 Act required that the ownership of all common land should be recorded. **(26)**

Malvern Hills Trust's web site shows a map of all they land they own. This includes additional land they purchased from private landowners, which is not common land. [27]

Concerns about Commoners Rights

The requirement for commoners rights to be registered coincided with the purchase of Castlemorton Common by the Conservators and this was probably the root cause of so much mistrust, some of which is still evident today. There was fear that the Conservators would in some way "change the rules" to the detriment of commoners, whereas in fact they were constrained legally by the Malvern Hills Acts and by the Commons Registration Act and they had, and still have, no choice but to comply with both, although there are some small grey areas of interpretation, particularly regarding the precise meaning of the right of estovers,[28] or where different parts of the Acts contradict each other,

The 1930 Malvern Hills Act gave the Conservators the power to make byelaws "providing nothing contained in this section or byelaw made thereunder shall prejudice or affect or take away any rights of common or commonable rights which are excerciseable by any person" except "for the regulating the user and enjoyment of any rights of common or commonable rights in accordance so far as may be with the ancient customs of the forest of Malvern or other customs under which such rights may be enjoyed".

More simply, as the Conservators web site shows in 2019, "they shall not do any thing or act which will take away or adversely affect the right of any commoner".

WORCESTER
SUMMER ASSIZES,
1810.

AT these Assizes a Cause was tried which excited considerable interest, wherein **EDWARD THOMAS FOLEY**, Esq. was *PLAINTIFF*, and **WILLIAM HARTLEY**, Esq. and another *DEFENDANTS.*—The gist of the Action was to try, *whether the Freeholders, Tenants, and Commoners, of the Parish of* GREAT MALVERN, *in this County, had* (in exclusion of Mr. FOLEY, as Lord of the Manor) *a right to Crop the Trees growing on the Waste Lands within the Parish.*

In support of this RIGHT, a Decree of the Court of Exchequer, so far back as the Reign of *King Charles the First*, with an Act of Parliament confirming it, was produced and ALLOWED by *Plaintiff's Counsel*, whereby the RIGHT was *clearly ascertained*, and PROOF of Mr. HARTLEY and his Ancestors' usage of Cropping adduced; but from an error in the Pleadings, a VERDICT was taken by the *Plaintiff*.

This decision does not vitiate the RIGHT of the Commoners, which, as before observed, *was clearly proved, and continues unimpeached.*

——ooooo——
PRINTED BY T. HOLL AND SON, WORCESTER.

Poster dated 1810.

Chapter 6

UNDER MALVERN HILLS CONSERVATORS
1965-2017

As early as May 1925 there had been rumours that the Conservators were going to take over the Common, but they came to nothing.

In 1963, the Conservators approached the Church Commissioners seeking to acquire Shadybank Common and Hangmans Hill [29] and purchased them the same year.

In July 1963, Castlemorton Parish Council had expressed an interest (to the Commissioner's solicitors), in buying Castlemorton Common (540 acres), but their offer was rejected. The Commissioners explained that it was not a matter of Parish Council needing to make a better offer, as the Commissioners had a preference for the Conservators to manage the common in future. The Parish Council decided not to pursue the purchase of the common as "it was obvious that Malvern Hills Conservators were going to be the new owners".

Contracts for the sale of Castlemorton Common to the Conservators were exchanged on 21 December 1964 at a price of £1459. The Church Commissioners retained mineral rights under the common and are still the Lord of the Manor. As the Chairman of the Conservators Hills and Quarries Committee, Edward Ballard, put it in 1965 "37 years of rule by Upton District Council and Castlemorton Parish Council has been to produce a weed ridden unsightly waste under no control at all." The Parish Council offered to continue to manage the common for two years under the existing bye-laws, but unsurprisingly this was rejected by the Conservators.

In 1966 the following article about the state of the common was published "You can go out to Castlemorton now and see, in spite of their bye-laws, an enormous number of things that clearly want attention of a conservator's board – derelict old cars, rubbish, encroachments. Quite the most serious thing I have seen however, is the traffic across the common. It is absolutely and utterly out of hand. Local people drive anywhere they like. Many acres have been cut up in this way," said Mr Ballard. Mr R H M Bartleet, said he had known the common since he was a boy and he did not consider there was a great a need to spend as much money on it as some people seem to think. "It is wild. It may be untidy. For the time being let it continue like that. Spend as little as possible on it. This tidying up idea I think can be taken too far. Let us stand on our rights legally, be very light-handed in imposing our rights and do the minimum until such time as it becomes apparent that something should be done", he said.

There was enormous local concern that the Conservators would seek to infringe commoners rights and would impose unworkable bye-laws, but both turned out to be completely unfounded. Essentially the problem was that the purchase of the common coincided with the registration of commoners rights, so there was a general atmosphere of mistrust. A Commoners Association was formed to defend the commoners rights of its members. Mr Davis Preece of Fairoaks Farm was appointed to call a meeting with a view to electing a committee.

There was considerable friction between the Parish Council, who regarded it as their responsibility to liaise with the Conservators, and the Commoners Association who did not trust either of them.

At the Parish Council meeting in March 1966, Percy Bunn called for a vote of no-confidence in the Parish Council, "95% of this parish have no confidence in your Council. You want throwing out neck and crop".

Mr A Ballard, Chairman of the Conservators, wrote "the main difficulty about the exercise of rights of pasture is that it does not pay. The Conservators have a definite interest in having stock on the commons to control vegetation and having done all they can, including obtaining bylaws as a basis on which the commoners can reorganise their methods. It is the view of many commoners in this district that unless quite a lot is done this particular method of agriculture will become extinct. I hope at least some of the Castlemorton commoners will realise that our interests are mutual." The same letter could have been written yesterday!

In 1969, the Conservators issued new bye-laws, which also covered the common, which were virtually the same as their existing ones.

The precept issue [30]

The Conservators now had responsibility for managing an additional 654 acres without a penny of new income to do so. One option they considered was to increase the level of precept on the existing precept payers [31].

There was another choice. The need to extend the precept had been anticipated in the 1884 Malvern Hills Act, Section 31, Provision for adding other common or waste lands. This empowered the Conservators to levy parishes in which they subsequently acquired common land, providing those were also give the right to appoint (or share in the appointment of) one or more Conservators. This was subject to the approval of the Land Commissioners (now defunct) and the Lord of the Manor. The Conservators have never exercised this right and in the proposed redrafting and consolidation of the Malvern Hills Acts this clause has been omitted without explanation.

The course of events is somewhat confusing [32]. The Conservators seem not to understand what powers they had to precept the new parishes in which they now held land [33] and they received conflicting advice. These parishes objected to being asked to pay and it was suggested that as people from all over Worcestershire enjoyed the common, Worcestershire County Council should be pressed to pay for the upkeep of the common. [34]

In the end, it all came to nothing and no levy has ever been made on Castlemorton Parish. Worcestershire County Council paid £10,400 in 2019, replacing the grant they had been paying via Upton Rural District Council prior to the common's acquisition by the Conservators.

Castlemorton Commoners Association [35]

The Commoners Association was formed in 1964 because there was a certain amount of feeling generated between some of the commoners, who thought that the Conservators might try to interfere with their rights, and some of the members of the Conservators Board, who perhaps felt that some of the commoners were simply dog-in-the-manger trouble makers! In fact nearly all the problems turned out to be imagined rather than real, and gradually the situation has improved, to the point where the annual meetings between the Malvern Hills Conservators, the local Parish Council and the Common Association Committee, are now very cordial, and always include a jolly session in the Robin Hood afterwards! [36]

There have been occasions when the Association has been involved in legal matters, for instance at the Registration hearings, when valuable assistance was given by Hr P Davis of Foster and Finlay, but today it serves as mainly a social organisation, arranging barn dances etc. and an annual gymkhana and shindig [37] which takes place on the common, alongside the soccer pitch at Hollybed.

In recent years, in view of the fact that the number of people actually exercising their common rights has declined, and the number of visitors to the common has increased, the Association has been "re-styled" to reflect the modern situation. It was decided to change the name to the Castlemorton Common Association [35] so that anybody interested in the common may become a member even if they do not have common rights. The Association makes occasional grants to the Conservators for specific areas to be cleared of overgrowth. Dick Dawe set up a rival organisation in the 1990s and from time to time asked the Parish Council for support, but it was felt that the terms of membership were unclear and it was not recognised.

Management of the Commons

Up until the 1990s burning had been used by the Conservators as a management tool to control the scrub. It followed the tradition of local farmers throwing a match in the bushes on their way to their home from the pub, a practice now prohibited under the bye-laws.

Med Snookes wrote in 1986 in his guidebook to Castlemorton Common: "More clearance of scrub, and mowing of grasses will obviously be necessary, as the "natural" controls are lost. The thistle problem illustrates this point. A certain number of thistles are desirable, because they do support a number of birds and insects but they can take over areas completely if left unchecked, to the detriment of other plant species. At the moment mowing of thistly areas in late autumn is sufficient to control them, because there is still enough help from the cattle and sheep, which will browse on young thistles, and also trample them. However in the future it may become necessary to also mow them in the early part of the year or to invest in subsidised grazing, or even to spray them, all of which are undesirable, but inevitable consequences of the changes which are taking place. It is hoped that enough people will graze enough stock for a long time yet.

The sheep are of several breeds, mainly cross-bred, with a large proportion of Suffolk blood, as well as crosses with Welsh, Kerry Hill, Border Leicester, Hill Radnor etc. [38] The cattle are also mixed, with Friesian, Hereford, Angus and Dairy Shorthorn being well represented. In winter, as long as the weather is not too hard, the cattle and sheep are turned out on the common to prevent the poaching up of the in-farm pasture by trampling. They forage about, finding what they can, but are brought in at night for feeding in the sheds or barns. Some cattle are turned out with their calves as single sucklers, and others are brought in at night for suckling calves kept in sheds on the farms.

The calves are sold off, when ready, as store cattle, i.e. for fattening up by farmers with more lush land. The ewes drop their lambs from the end of February onwards and today most are brought in for lambing, but there are still some which give birth on the common - a rare sight for visitors from town. During the winter, hay etc is sometimes put out on the common during the day to keep the sheep near home. It is often thrown on the gorse to encourage the animals to keep it grazed down a bit. After lambing, the ewes and lambs are turned out on the common again, during the day, as before. It is usually about May when a good "bite" develops on the common and until this time, bringing in at night and feeding close to home is important to prevent straying. Shearing and dipping is carried out in early June and most of the lambs are sold, again as store-lambs, between August and September. Some time after the sale of the lambs, the ewes go to the ram, or tup, for mating which is timed as far as possible to produce the lambs after the worst of the winter."

The increase in overgrowth on the Common has been a longstanding local issue, exacerbated by the reduction in grazing. A local resident who moved into the area in the 1970s remembers that the Hancocks Lane side was all grass, no gorse, bramble or trees. Since about 2005 a programme of clearance had been instigated, even on the SSSI, and in 2016 a formal Land Management Plan was adopted. In recent years the Conservators have made use of government grant schemes including Higher Level Stewardship to manage the common and support sensitive livestock grazing.

An undated early publication by Malvern Hill Conservators quotes the grazing levels for cattle on the

Commons as approximately 50, and sheep grazing the hills as having declined from 1,500 prior to 1960, to 850 in 1966 and 550 in 1979/80. [39]

In anticipation that those remaining graziers would eventually retire or give up, the Conservators now have the power to licence any person to put any animal on the common.

All cattle and sheep on the common are identified with a mark to show to whom they belong.

Yellow	Barbara Wilkes
Red	Roy Shails
Green	Matt Gardner
Blue	Dermot Weaver
Purple	Chris Ball

Management Plans

Before 2006, the Conservators vision was to "To maintain Castlemorton Common as an area of special landscape and wildlife value which can be enjoyed by local people and visitors as an area for quiet recreation, whilst enabling those with common rights to utilise the common as part of their farming practice in a viable and sustainable manner".

Legally, they could hardly do otherwise.

In October 2005, The Malvern Hills Heritage Partnership (funded by the Heritage Lottery Fund) engaged a firm called Land Use Consultants to independently review the issues affecting Castlemorton Common and draw up an action plan for the next 10 years. This was published in October 2006.

The management of the SSSI changed in about 2010

when cutting mowing was allowed and much overgrown space opened up to the public.

The Trust now regularly publishes its plans for managing the common, allowing time for consultation.

Castlemorton Commons Co-ordinating Committee [40]

Known as the 4C's, this was established in 2007 principally to give advice on the Higher Level Stewardship awards, as well as to provide a forum for discussion about the management of Castlemorton, Hollybed and Coombe Green commons. The aim of Higher Level Stewardship is for farmers to undertake environmental management schemes which offer "significant benefits" to high-priority areas. Funding comes from DEFRA (Department for Environment, Food and Rural Affairs) and is managed locally on their behalf by Malvern Hills Conservators.

The committee meets three times a year and its constitution and minutes are published on Malvern Hills Conservators web site.

Area of Outstanding Natural Beauty [41]

In 1949, the National Parks and Countryside Act sought to protect areas of outstanding natural beauty and in 1959 40 square miles of an area including the Malvern Hills was so designated. In 2007, all land to west of Gloucester Road in the Parish of Castlemorton, together with a small area of common to the East of Gloucester Road near Welland, became part of the AONB.

Map of Parishes in the AONB.

Ongoing problems with cars

The public roads across the common are the responsibility of Worcestershire County Council and fall under police jurisdiction. The Conservators have no power to deal with parking or speeding on these roads.

There are many tracks across the common providing access to properties, and these are maintained by the owners of the properties using approved materials. The legal right for owners of residential properties to drive across the common for access is determined either by a Deed of Grant from the Conservators, or by Prescriptive Rights – proof of access for at least the last 20 years.

On common land owned by the Conservators, it is

contrary to the bye-laws for an unauthorised person to drive a motor vehicle on the common. Visitors will see signs at the start of access tracks indicating that they are not for public use.

One of several types of information notices for visiting motorists.

Active graziers may take agricultural vehicles onto the common where it is necessary to do so in order to look after their animals.

In about 2001, the former parking area next to the Gullet Quarry was closed off, with access only for residents. The Conservators explained "This beauty spot has had all kinds of problems over the years. The Conservators along with the community have thought long about how to help this exquisite area of the Hills regain an air of calm. By closing the car park and having the lane open only to residents' traffic the approach to the Gullet will be a pleasant flat walk. To compensate a new surfaced car park is proposed at Swinyard Hill".

Swinyard Car Park was created in 2002. [42]

Legal Matters

For several years there was concern amongst those who needed to drive across the common to reach their properties. When these properties were being sold, the purchaser's solicitor was insisting on Deed of Grant, to be obtained and paid for by the vendor. [43] The Countryside and Rights of Way Act 2000 required the Conservators to charge a scale of fees for a Deed of Grant, up to 2% of the value of the premises. The then owners of one property bounding the common had to pay over £8,000 for their Deed of Grant. The Conservators did not wish to make these higher charges and made a request to the Charity Commission to be able to waive them, which was declined. Following a challenge in the House of Lords in 2002, the requirement to charge a fee was over-ruled and the scale fee regulations were repealed by the Commons Act 2006. [44] Today, the only charge made is one to cover the administrative costs involved.

The 2002 Land Registration Act encouraged the owners of Common Land to register their holdings with the Land Registry. Malvern Hills Conservators did so in 2006.

Jonnie Hart [45]

In the early 1980s, a local man called John or Jonnie Hart lived rough on the common. He would support himself with eggs, milk and hens from local farms. At one time, he lived in the barn on what is now Dermot Weaver's land near Shadybank Common and also in a hut in The Roughs. Dermot Weaver remembers as a young boy going to the barn at night with a tilley lamp to help with lambing. When he lit the lamp, John Hart's face appeared out of the darkness and startled him.

Dermot remembers him saying very little, mainly grunting if you tried to engage in conversation. He could not read or write. Tim Cameron from Dales Hall remembers John Hart foraging for cherries in his garden and also that he was fond of blackberries. Tim remembers that he had a large lump on his head. He also slept in a wooden hut at Hollybush quarry. Another family recalls finding him investigating the contents of their chest freezer and inviting him in for lunch (an event not to be repeated). Another resident remembers being startled by him as he emerged within a barn near Castlemorton School. She thought he might have sometimes lived in the ruin of a house just up Heron Lane, which she knew as Hart's Lane. He is now cared for in a Worcestershire nursing home.

Chapter 7

THE CASTLEMORTON RAVE
(22 - 29 MAY 1992)

Written by Mary Watts

On the afternoon of the Friday before the Spring Bank Holiday in May 1992 the Gloucestershire police moved on a group of new age travellers who had parked up in a lay by near Moreton Valence on the A38. The motley caravan of old buses, converted trucks and caravans was moved over the county boundary into Worcestershire. Somehow they ended up parking on Castlemorton Common. Word was passed on and by the evening the camp was growing as more and more partygoers arrived. The sound systems had been set up around the crossroads on the Gullet road and the heavy bass beats were audible for miles around.

Avon and Somerset police had put Operation Nomad into action to prevent a repetition of the Avon Free festivals held on previous May bank holidays near Bristol. This had caused a great deal of noise and nuisance and the police force was under pressure to avoid it happening again. Operation Nomad was successful, but just shifted the problem to a new location. By the Saturday evening up to 40,000 people were on Castlemorton Common and the rave became the largest free festival since ones on Stonehenge in the early 1980s.

Spiral Tribe was at the centre of the organising the event. They were a collective of musicians, artists, rappers and DJs who put on free parties all over the country. These parties were intended to be open to all and represented the group's

The Rave from the air.

political resistance to private ownership of land, amongst other things. Other sound systems, including Bedlam, Circus Warp and the DIY Sound System also came to the party, along with big name DJs, and the immediate high profile media coverage attracted more ravers from all parts of the country. The rapid increase in numbers made it impossible for the authorities to close it down, much to the dismay of local residents. It was front page news on all national newspapers and covered extensively on television news programmes, provoking debate about the inadequacies of police powers to deal with the unauthorised festival.

The arrival of so many people on the common, with cars parked anyhow along the narrow approach roads, had a quite traumatic effect on the local residents. There was 24 hour music, people moving around all hours of the day and night, semi feral dogs roaming, wood being taken for campfires, and the police seemed to be incapable of keeping order. There were reports of lambs being savaged by the loose dogs, hens taken for eating, fences broken down, graffiti painted on walls, stones thrown through windows and shoplifting done at Welland Shop. Locals were frightened and threatened to retaliate. The SAS were brought in and used to ambush at least one drugged up raver who attacked a policeman in a resident's garden.

Services were laid on for the benefit of the travellers in an effort to keep them in Castlemorton rather than going into the towns. Malvern Hills District Council provided bin bags and social security benefits were delivered to the site. National newspapers and broadcasters sent reporters and photographers and the rave was front page news for the week it lasted. Once they had gone, a big effort was needed to clean up the site including litter, human excrement and drug equipment. Members of the Spiral Tribe sound system were charged with public order offences, but were not convicted and went on organising parties on the continent.

The rave and its disruption led to the passing of the Criminal Justice and Public Order Act 1994. The Bill was introduced by Michael Howard, Home Secretary of Prime Minister John Major's Conservative government, and attracted widespread opposition. The Labour Party abstained from voting for it. The Act introduced a number of changes to the existing law, particularly in the restriction and reduction of existing rights and in greater penalties for certain "anti-social" behaviours. It effectively made illegal outdoor rave parties that played music. Part V of the Act covers collective trespass and nuisance on land and includes sections against raves and further sections against disruptive trespass, squatters and unauthorised campers – most significantly the criminalisation of previously civil offences.

There are numerous videos of the event on YouTube.

Chapter 8

UNDER MALVERN HILLS TRUST FROM 2017

In 2017, Malvern Hills Conservators, with permission from the Charity Commission, adopted the working name Malvern Hills Trust.

In 2017, a scheme was piloted on Hollybed Common to cut bracken and turn it into brackettes which can be burnt on log fires. It was to be repeated in 2018 on Hollybed and Malvern Common.

Malvern Hill Trust's free map 'Walking and Cycling on the Malvern Hills' (published in 2018) shows well established footpaths and tracks across the common. It is available from the Trust's offices at Manor House, Grange Road, Malvern (opposite Malvern Theatre).

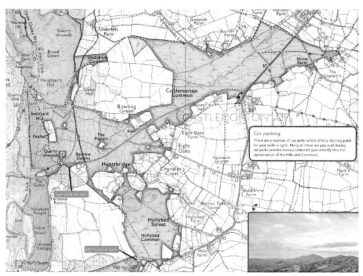

2018, well established footpaths and tracks.

In 2020, New Zealand Pygmyweed was identified in the ponds on Castlemorton Common. This non-native aquatic plant can grow into dense mats which smother native pond flora and fauna. The Trust are trialling the use of black polythene to exclude light form the pond to kill the plant. The plastic will remain in place for 2-3 years.

2021, Pond by Berrow Downs,
drained to kill off New Zealand Pygmyweed.

A second non-native invasive species was suspected to be living in the pond outside Mount Pleasant. Contractors discovered a healthy population of swan mussels. Some of the fish (bream, roach, rudd) caught during the survey were removed from the overstocked pond to restore a balance and create a healthier aquatic ecosystem.

In 2020, a watering point was established on Castlemorton Common to assist graziers.

Watering point.

In November 2019, around 70 cattle and 500 sheep were grazing the common and numbers seem to have stabilised around that. The Higher Level Stewardship Scheme, which included Coombe Green Common, ended on 31 March 2020. A new application for Castlemorton Common on its own, submitted in April 2021, and the new scheme started in February 2022. The Trust subsidised the graziers in the meanwhile.

In 2021, Western Power underground infrastructure leaked oil on the eastern side of Swinyard Hill. To protect the locale helicopters were used to remove the contaminated soil, replacing it with safe inert soil as guided by the Environment Agency. Swinyard Car Park was temporarily closed to act as a depot.

In November 2021, the Trust announced it was indefinitely suspending the issue of licences for trail hunting. This followed similar decisions by other major public landowners. The decision was taken because of the hunt's persistent failure to follow the conditions associated with the permission to allow them on Malvern Hills Trust's land.

Consolidating and updating the Malvern Hills Acts

In 2017 Malvern Hills Conservators adopted the working title of Malvern Hills Trust, as the start of program of modernisation. The five Acts of Parliament controlling the Trust were considered to be out of date and in need of overhaul.

During 2018, a series of public meetings were held around the area, including three at Castlemorton Parish Hall - which were well attended.

Working through the Charity Commission, a new scheme was drawn up to replace the previous five Acts. It was to be designed to be easier to follow, to remove obsolete references, resolve a few contradictions and incorporate new powers, and update the structure of the governing Board.

So far as the common was concerned, the proposed new powers included the power to:

Buy, own and sell livestock and all things for their care on common land.

Install cattle grids and permanent fences.

Erect temporary fences for up to 60 days for grazing purposes.

Erect temporary fences for up to 12 months for land and stock management.

It was recognised that more grazing was still required to maintain the common and that the future of the existing graziers was uncertain. It was unlikely that any new graziers with commoners rights would wish to exercise these, at least not with any great number of animals. With the present Higher Level Subsidy Payments Scheme ending in 2020 and no news of any proposed continuation, existing graziers might withdraw if grazing without subsidy was uneconomical. As a last resort, the Trust needed the power to put their own animals on the Common.

There was a belief that more graziers might come forward if the common could be secured. It was not possible to erect permanent fencing all around the common, as common land cannot be enclosed. However, the placing of cattle grids, with permanent fencing (with access gates) would prevent cattle straying onto the roads and out of the immediate area. This, together, with a very limited amount of permanent fencing, would largely secure the common and make stock easier to manage. This could be attractive to external graziers, who could be issued licences to graze by the Trust.

As Rob Havard, Conservation Officer for Malvern Hills Conservators, wrote in 2007 "One of the most important aspects of the grazing is that it helps to keep the scrub under control. While scrub is valued as a habitat in its own right, it needs to be managed in order for it to be maintained in good condition for wildlife. Cutting with machinery alone would not provide the diversity of plant structure necessary for many of the plants and invertebrates and would change the character of the common. The grazing also provides a really useful food source for young birds and also for the rare bats in the area that feed on the insects associated with animal dung".

Under the existing five Acts the Trust has no power to erect permanent fencing. Owners of common land throughout the rest of the country who are regulated by the general law relating to common land, do have the power to erect permanent fencing (subject to permission from The Secretary of State and a Public Enquiry). It is the special case of Castlemorton Common being managed under its own Acts of Parliament, that failed to include such a power, and that limited the Trust.

The Trust already has power to erect temporary fencing and this is actively used to restrict cattle to certain areas of the common at certain times of the year. Especially, it is used to assist in the management if the SSSI.

The Trust also planned to change their legally incorporated name from Malvern Hills Conservators to Malvern Hills Trust.

The draft of the new scheme was first sent to the Charity Commission and in January 2019 was sent out of for local discussion and comment. A summary of comments was to be submitted to the Charity Commission in February 2020. As a result of the significant interest of precept payers the Charity Commission said the Trust could not proceed by way of a Charity Commission Scheme. This means that now a new Act can only be created by a private Bill through Parliament.

Chapter 9

THE MILL POND – GOLDEN VALLEY

A watercourse connects the Mill Pond to the ponds on Mill Farm and then flows through Longdon Brook to the river Severn. There was a corn mill at Mill Farm in 1885, so the Mill Pond acted as a header tank or pound to feed their ponds with water for the mill.

There is a sluice gate on the edge of the bund and water could have been released through underground pipes (hence the discontinuity between the stream and the pond) into the stream which then became a leet.

The 1812 Ordnance Survey map shows the outflow through only a northern stream, so the southern branch operated by a sluice must have been installed between 1813 and 1839, and then the northern stream blocked off.

1812 Ordnance Survey Map.

In 1839, the Mill Pond (and Mill Farm) was owned by Charles Porter of The Mythe, Tewkesbury. The Porter family were long established wealthy landowners and Charles Porter was elected Mayor of Tewkesbury on 11 November 1841.

By 1869, 1 April, the Upper Mill Pond had become detached from Mill Farm and was still owned by the Porter family.

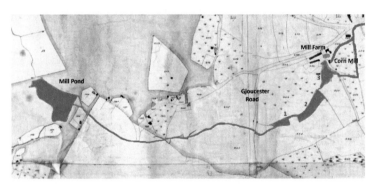

The Tithe Map (1839) shows three ponds, fed from the Mill Pond on Golden Valley, and the site of the Corn Mill. By 1904 the Corn Mill was disused, although all three ponds remained. By 1923, pond 2 was half marsh ground and by 1955 ponds 1 and 2 had gone completely. Today, only pond 3 remains and this was de-silted in 2016.

In 1877, 5 October, the Church Commissioners bought the Mill Pond (3 acres, 0 rods, 11 perches) from the Trustees of the marriage settlement of Catherine Porter (Charles's daughter) to Frederick Gerard of Kinwarton Hall, Warwickshire. They married on 29 April 1869. At the same time, the Church Commissioners bought Mill Farm.

In 1952, a letter from M Arthur describes the pond as being in 'a bad state' and Parish Council minutes in 1955 and 1956 record the need to repair the dam.

In 1957, Leonard Bunn, Chairman of Castlemorton Parish Council, issued a letter asking for donations to repair the dam. R Shails was authorised to receive donations, with £45:5:10d already in the account.

In 1958, District Council was requested by the Church Commissioners to fence off the dam at the bottom of the common to protect the public. The Commissioners would pay half the cost and the District Council seemed to expect the Parish Council to pay the other half. The Church Commissioners also offered to make a substantial payment towards the repair of the dam, providing the Parish Council took responsibility for it thereafter and in October the Parish Council agreed to that proposal but appear not to have followed through. There was even some concern that the pond might have to be drained permanently to avoid prevent future costs.

In 1960, the Surveyor from Upton Rural District Council wrote to Castlemorton Parish Council to say that he was taking steps to fence off the dam because of its dangerous condition.

Jakemans swimming in the Mill Pond, date unknown.

The Church Commissioners sold the pond to Upton District Council on 10 March 1961, who, by September, had constructed a new dam. The agreement was that the new dam would be paid for as follows: Parish Council £50, County Council £441:2s, Church Commissioners £370.

The Parish Council were asked to help deal with the

The Dam, August 2017.

provision for car parking, as the District Council had no power to do this themselves.

In 1968 the Conservators made an approach to purchase the pond and the District Council confirmed they had no plans to sell it. The Parish Council confirmed they had no interest in having any delegated powers regarding the Millpond.

However, there were ongoing costs to be faced. There was uncertainty over who would keep the banks under repair – the District Council or the Conservators. The pond was badly silted and lily growth was getting out of hand, requiring some £500 to £600 to be expended. There was local concern that if the Conservators took it over, fishing rights and stock watering rights might be under threat. [46]

In December 1968 it was decided to offer the Conservators a 21 year lease for £1 per annum, which they took up on 21 January 1971. [47]

9 August 1939.

In 1987, it was dredged it and the spoil was used to fill in the old gravel working pits to the south, which is why the land there is now so level.

In 1994, 6 September, it was purchased by the Conservators. In about 2005-2010 the dam was strengthened with substantial repair works.

The pond is home to two breeds of geese: white domestic geese and Canada geese. There are a few cross-bred domestic/Canada geese amongst them. Visitors are asked not to feed the geese.

Chapter 10

MILITARY AND WAR

Training on the common

From 1875 and until 1892, military training for Artillery Volunteers was being undertaken with an annual camp at Castlemorton. These were big affairs with up to 1,000 men and 40lb guns being fired. Sometimes this was on private land and sometimes on the common itself, as in 1884 we read that "Last year the tents were pitched on Castlemorton Common, but this was found inconvenient, as the common being open the visitors could not be kept out of the camp". Used shells are still occasionally found today. One local resident has them adorning his garden.

In August 1885 there was an Artillery Encampment on the common. During the week heavy gun-practice with 40-pounder breechloading Armstrongs had been carried on over a range of 3,000 yards, the targets being placed at the rabbit-warren, at the top of Castlemorton Common, "The Worcester Division did some excellent practice on Thursday striking the target twice", we are told.

The reporting of the annual camps year after year followed a similar format. [48] A list of all the local dignitaries who attended, praise for the troops, an account of what they did and the results of any competitions. [49]

After 1892 it was decided to seek a new venue [50], but by 1900, they were back on the common again.

In 1902, Madresfield Yeomanry camp men had a field day

at Castlemorton Common, where they were instructed in various tactical exercises, such as the attack in skirmishing order, etc. In the afternoon there was a special parade for the purpose selecting the best turned-out horses in each squadron and for the regiment.

A minute from the Parish Council records that the Resolution of 13 January 1914 should have attention from the War Office stating that Castlemorton was included in the areas of Army manoeuvres of 1916 laid before the Council.

During World War 1, Shady Bank common was used for heavy artillery practice.

World War II

The Agricultural Development Act was passed in 1939 and War Agricultural Executive Committees (War Ags) were re-formed to determine land usage. At the start of the war, the County War Agricultural Executive Committee directed that all available land should be ploughed to grow corn. Worcestershire War Agricultural Committee had to find 26,000 acres of grassland to plough, of which 5,000 was for potatoes.

Appreciation was expressed to the commoners for their ready co-operation in withdrawing their cattle and placing the commons at the disposal of the War Agricultural Committee and agreeing to the ploughing up. They probably had no choice as their land was requisitioned.

A newspaper article recorded "We might as well tell our grandchildren that in those days when the British Empire stood resolute to fight on, alone if need be, for the right of mankind to live in freedom when it was touch and go.

The lighter field on the right below Foxhall was ploughed. Note the fence on the left hand side to keep the cattle off it.

Another view of ploughed land below Foxhall.

Ploughed land viewed from Mount Pleasant.

Hereward Weaver at Mount Pleasant. A crop on the common can be seen to the right, in the background.

Pig sties at Mount Pleasant with crops in the background. Looking towards the Malvern Hills.

Castlemorton Common was enabled to "do its bit" in yields up to 26 cwt of corn per acre, to help eke out the country's scanty rations."

The extent of land which had been requisitioned by the Agricultural Executive Committee was confirmed as: Quarry Piece, 60 acres, burnt off and ploughed in the summer and limed, and used for oats. Hurst Bank, 30 acres and Mount Pleasant, 20 acres. Hurst Bank came first in April 1949, when it was fenced off on the West side with barbed wire, with gates for Rose Cottage, Bakers Farm and Hurst Farm. After the war, cereal crops and potatoes were grown on Hurst Bank. I am grateful to Roger Jakeman for indicating the areas marked on the following maps.

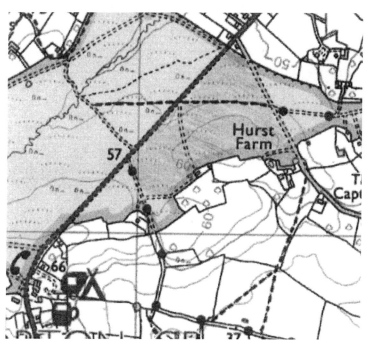

Hurst Bank. (Magic Maps base map)

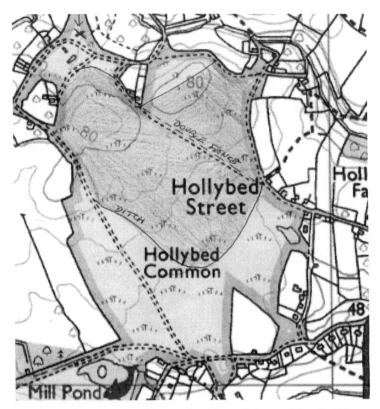

Hollybed Common. The site of a Nissen Hut used by the War Ag to store tools is marked with a red cross. It was sold when the common was reinstated. A double fence followed the line of the modern track, separating the common into two.

(Magic Maps, base map)

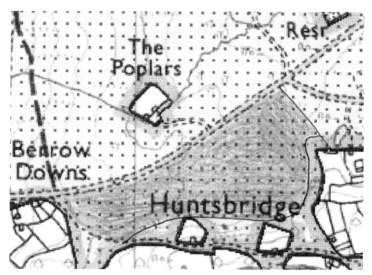

Mount Pleasant. (Magic Maps base map)

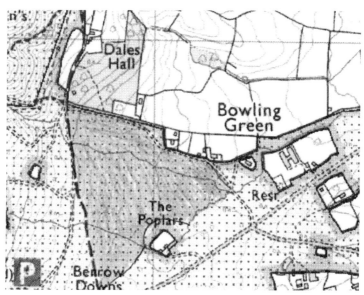

Quarry Piece. (Magic Maps base map)

Robert Weaver, writing in 1958, recounts how the lower part of Upper Common and Coppice Flat (Shady Bank Common) had been cleared. The late Mr William Whittle ploughed out and cleared Hollybed Common; Robert's brother William Weaver and his eldest son ploughed and cleared Lower Common from Gorse Bank to Narrow Hedges (near the land the Conservators bought to the southeast of Shady Bank Common, adjoining Weaver's land). All this was done without charge.

By 1942 almost the whole of Hollybed and Upper Commons were ploughed, also a substantial part of Lower Common. Yields were up to 50 bushels per acre, compared with 130-190 per acres for normal farming. More could have been ploughed, but it was set aside for cattle.

In 1947, 54 acres of Hollybed common were released and re-seeded. The yield had been 17-18 cwt per acre. The rest of the land was still required for wheat, but it was hoped to release 20 acres of Mount Pleasant and 74 acres of Hollybed in 1949, and the remaining 50 acres in 1950. Hollybed and Mount Pleasant were to be in ley for a year and then the grass was to be cut and sold by auction, as had been done on the Quarry Piece. Then they were to be '"bastard fallowed", planted with corn and seeded with permanent pasture in 1948 ready to be handed back in 1949.

A petition to the local Member of Parliament followed in 1948, asking for the rest of the land to be released.

In April 1950 Hurst Bank, which had been reseeded in 1946, was released and quickly began to deteriorate to its former state, due to insufficient cropping. Other land was held until its maximum date, December 1952, because it was "still capable of growing worthwhile arable crops".

In September 1952, the War Ag wrote to the Parish Council regarding the re-seeding of Hollybed common and elsewhere. It needed the commoners to keep the animals off the re-seeded areas. In August the seeding had been shooting, but was now being grazed by sheep. Although the common had not been handed back, they assumed that the commoners were satisfied with the re-seeding.

In 1955, there was a plan to requisition Shady Bank Common for not more than 28 days annually for 5 years as a temporary training area. Two officers and 40 from the ranks would be firing blank rounds. They needed to dig 6 pits, 11ft by 2ft, and these would be covered over. The ground would be reinstated at the end of the five years. Permission was refused.

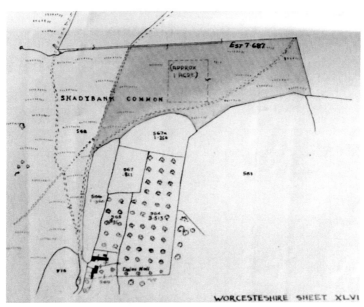

The 1 acre to be requisitioned for training.

In 1958, quotations were sought for liming the common, in readiness for derequisitioning. It was eventually returned to open common land and re-seeded. The quality of the new grass was too good for animals accustomed to poor quality grazing and many suffered with bloating.

Quotations were received from Southmead Motor Company of Bristol, Worcestershire Farmers and Laird Agricultural Services of Malvern for supply and spreading. The ph (acidity/alkalinity) of the commons was tested and Windalls & Clutterbucks (Quarry Piece) was 4.0, requiring 4 tons per acre; Hurst and Hollybed 5.6 needing 2 tons per acre. The work had to be done urgently as a subsidy was available and about to expire. Castlemorton Common required 100 tons.

Searchlight

A searchlight was set up on common by the Gullet Road, opposite the road down to Eight Oaks to spot enemy aircraft. An outline of the searchlight base can still be seen and is also visible on Google Earth. There are also brick foundations of related buildings close by. The Parish Council wrote to the RA Battery in 1941 requesting its removal and Captain CC Stubbing replied "it is not possible for the emplacements on the site to be filled in as it is not yet known if the site is to be permanently vacated. Arrangements are being made for the emplacements to be adequately fenced in order to prevent danger to cattle etc. Immediately orders are received to abandon the site the holes will be completely filled in".

Historic England lists the searchlight remains and also a World War II machine gun and spigot mortar and blacker bombard firing range from corner of the road to the Gullet and Gloucester Road and Territorial Army firing training ground just south west of Strawbyn Bridge.

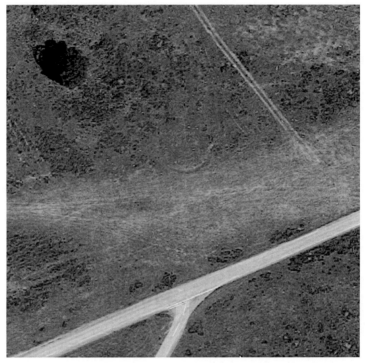

Searchlight base – circle in the centre of the picture.

Roger Jakeman remembers his father driving across the Welland straight with an empty stone lorry and seeing a light plane land on the common, on the hills side of Gloucester Road. As a result, 20ft poles were erected to prevent enemy planes landing there.

The Common was also used as a shooting range for practice, with slit trenches dug and Free French and Belgian troops taking part. A red flag was raised and sentries stood on guard.

After the war the Parish Council gave permissions for

military camps and training. No fires and no live ammunition were allowed:

1952, Worcestershire Territorial Army, 8 light wheeled vehicles

1956, Worcester Royal Grammar School CCF training field day

1958, RRE barrage balloon flying at 2000 feet

1959, RRE 'certain aerial measurements' using two vehicles

1959, 22nd Special Air Service Regiment, Malvern, parachute jumping

1960, 1st Battalion Worcester Regiment technical exercises

1962, Bromsgrove School CCF training field day

1964, 7th Battalion Royal Worcester Regiment, camping on common for training

Chapter 11

ARCHAEOLOGY AND FEATURES

The Commons are a site of archaeological interest. The poor quality of the soil was a disincentive to cultivation, especially ploughing (except during World War II), and this has helped to preserve many of the historic features. Thirteen sites are listed by Worcestershire County Council Archaeology Section, but most are mounds, ditches and earthworks of unknown age. There has been no archaeological excavation and there is little firm evidence to positively interpret them. There are also listings by Historic England which may be viewed through the Heritage Gateway: www.heritagegateway.org.uk/Gateway/. Use UK Grid Reference Finder to see each location on a map.

There are verbal reports of musket balls and cannon balls being found on Shady Bank Common.

The 1885 Ordnance Survey maps show various features, including quarries and clays pits (known locally as Marly Holes). The main features are shown below.

A sheepwash on the south of Hancocks Lane by Tippers Patch.

85

Site of the sheepwash.

Sheepwash by the gate to Hancock's Lane,
identified through local knowledge.

Old gravel pit near Yew Tree House,
named Yew Tree Cottage on this 1887 map.

Site of the old gravel pit near Yew Tree House.

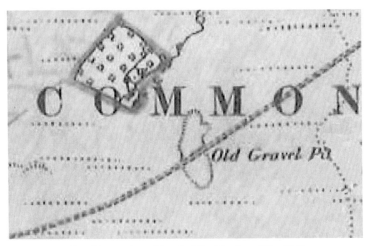

*An old gravel working by The Poplars (No 584),
on either side of the Gullet Road.*

The brown vegetation marks the old gravel working near The Poplars.

The brown vegetation marks the old gravel working near The Poplars.

Chandlers Cross, where New Road joins Common Road.
Believed to be an old Marl Pit, as an earlier name of
Mouchers Corner was Marl Cottage.

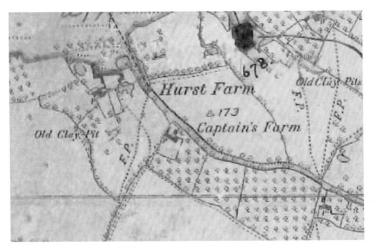

Old clay pit near Hurst Farm.

Site of the saw pit in The Cut, near where Castlemorton Common joins Coombe Green Common.

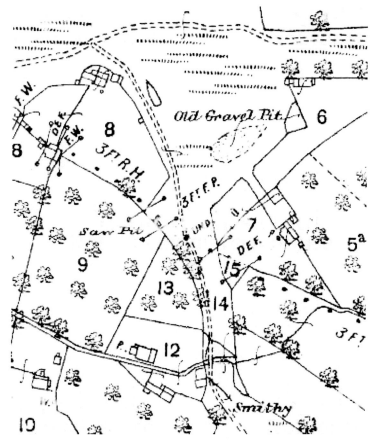

A saw pit and old gravel pit on the track south on Golden Valley.

Site of old gravel working showing Straights House Cottage in the background and the track to Little Orchards.

The Football Pitch on Hollybed Common. It is always dry as it sits on natural gravel.

Marl Pool on Hollybed Common.

The Marl Pool or Bomb Pool on Hollybed Common. There is a story circulating that this was made by a German bomber shedding bombs to lose weight as it approached the hills, but Roger Jakeman says that as a child it was always known as the Marley Pool – where marl had been extracted – and the other story is fiction. The structure strongly suggests it was a marl pit.

Ditch on Hollybed Common. This marks the southern limit of cultivation in World War II.

X *marks the location of boundary stone. There is a green marker post in the ground to help you find it. A survey in 1823 indicates this as a "Boundary Stone of the Warren". It is believed to relate to the Rabbit Warren belonging to Thomas Charles Gandolphi Hornyhold.*

Boundary stone on Hangman's Hill, showing initials interpreted as Thomas C(harles) H(ornihold)M(alvern).

The old track continuing parallel to the Hills after descending from Dales Hall and turning towards Swinyard Car Park. It was described by Robert Weaver in about 1960 and called the Border Way and continued across Hollybed Common to the old mill.

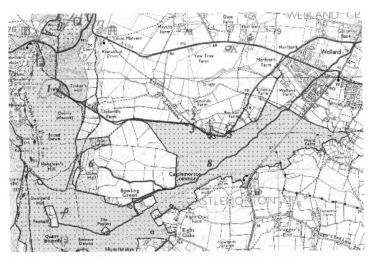

Marlbank Brook. (Magic Maps base map)

The brook flows from British Camp reservoir (1) coming on to the common at Gate Cottage (2) on Hancocks Lane. It passes through the locally identified sheepwash (3), behind the island of privately owned piece of land surrounded by the common known as Tippers Patch (4), through the old sheepwash and leaves the common at Springbank Cottage (5). It continues on to cross Gloucester Road north of Welland and eventually joins the River Severn.

A smaller stream joins the Brook at Welland. It is fed from separate sources near Broomhill Coppice (6) and near Foxhall (7). There is a small bridge across it opposite Hunters Hall (8) and the streams flows through a large pipe some distance west where the common meets privately owned land.

After years of problems with water shortages plans were made in 1890 to build the British Camp reservoir at a cost of £26,000. The 1891 Malvern Water Act allowed the reservoir to be built and, in 1895, it was opened by the Princess Mary,

The bridge over the stream opposite Hunters Hall, extended in 2020. The bridge was certainly there in 1927 when the owner of Fairfield, George Hamblin, was paid for work on it.

the Duchess of York. Severn Trent are required to maintain a flow of water of 28,000 gallons of water a day into Marlbank Brook. This is achieved by releasing about 3" of water from the reservoir, less if it has rained as the rainwater contributes towards the flow.

We may also deduce that the brook across the common had a decent flow of water for many years, as in 1830 one Benjamin Barnett, aged about 80, fell into the brook across Castlemorton Common and was drowned.

The stream running through a pipe. The ground here used to be very boggy and rutted by agricultural vehicle tracks.

Chapter 12

GEOLOGY, FLORA AND FAUNA

Geology

This section has been taken from a booklet was originally written and published in 1986 by Med Snookes and I am grateful to Val Snookes for permission to reproduce it. Other passages from the booklet have been incorporated into the relevant chapters.

Castlemorton Common has survived until the present time because of its geological history. Britain can be divided into Highland and Lowland regions, by drawing a curved line from the mouth of the River Exe in Devon, to the mouth of the River Tees in Yorkshire. The Malvern Hills form part of this line, and it is strange, but true, that even though the highest point is only just over 1300 feet above sea level, the next equal height due north east is the Ural mountains of Central Russia, 4,000 miles away.

The rocks of the hill ridge are very ancient, being pushed up into the earth's crust over 500 million years ago, in the Cambrian period. These rocks were covered by a sea in

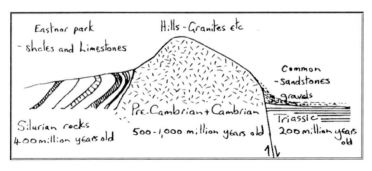

Silurian times, about 400 million years ago, and later an earth movement, known as the Cheltenham drive, pushed up the hills as a ridge, whilst creating a fault along the eastern side. As the sedimentary Silurian rocks were eroded, the hills were left as a ridge by Triassic times about 200 million years ago.

The climate of the Triassic period was that of a very harsh desert. The Keuper sandstones were built up over the landscape to the east of the hills, i.e. where the common is now. Thus the scene was set, as shown in the diagram.

During the Great Ice Age, which ended only about 10,000 years ago, an ice-sheet extended from the north down as far as Gloucester, and the Malvern Hills probably stuck up through as bare frost-shattered peaks.

When the ice sheets began to melt, they deposited glacial clay and boulders. However no deposits of this clay have yet been found east of the hills, but the whole area within a mile or two of them has deposits of Malvernian gravels, especially thick in some areas on the lower flanks of the actual hill slopes. These gravels are basically all the frost-shattered bits of rock, which were washed down by melt waters or gradually crept down the bare hills under the influence of gravity.

The hill soil is too thin and acid, and the gravels are difficult to cultivate being relatively infertile. This fact led to the survival of the commons, the more fertile soils of the river terraces being used in preference and the area around the hills was left as wilderness. The solid geology can be seen in the Gullet quarry, and the gravels in the banks of the stream in the middle of the common

The main natural vegetation of Britain is forest, and after the Ice Age, the plants slowly returned, until most of the country was covered in a blanket of trees, but it was a blanket full of holes. So it was in this area, when prehistoric man first arrived, as a hunter, and found the bare hill tops, and thick woodland, with some clearings where the soil was too stony, or wet, for trees to grow well. It is said that the name Malvern comes from the Celtic Moel Bryn meaning 'bareheaded'.

As Britain was settled man made little impact upon the area of the common, though there are Iron Age Hillforts on the hills either side - British Camp and Midsummer Hill, and the Romans built roads to the east and west. The only marks of man from this long period may be the ancient trackways across the waste, especially the old hill crossing by Pink Cottage. The old hollow ways leading from the car park by the Pink Cottage track, up through the bracken and through the Pink Cottage gap (which is called the Silurian pass in geological circles) probably date from this period, but the straight roads and tracks across the lower common, seem to be from the Mediaeval period rather than the Roman.

Flora and Fauna

When looking at the common today, it should be remembered that it is much more open than it used to be. Man gradually used up the woodland for fuel, fences and buildings. Grazing animals have prevented the regrowth of trees, by simply eating the seedlings or trampling them. This is reflected in the way that trees have begun to colonise parts of the land, as the number of grazing animals has dwindled. That part of the common by Hancocks Lane, where a thick scrub growth gives shelter to seedling trees, is rapidly reverting to woodland, and the preservation of open common is becoming a headache for the Malvern Hills Conservators, especially where they cannot use a tractor drawn mower.

The vegetation of the common varies greatly, depending on how wet the soil is, the aspect and steepness of the slopes, how heavily it is grazed or used by tourists, whether it was ploughed during the war, or dug for gravel etc. A large part of the Welland end of the common has been declared as an SSSI (Site of Special Scientific Interest), mainly because of the many rare-plants. There are at least 200 varieties including tubular water dropwort, lousewort, petty whim, heather and carline thistle, as well as the commoner sorts such as bluebell and primrose. The fauna of the hills and common is also very varied, and many insects, butterflies and beetles etc, which are generally rare in the West Midlands, are found here.

Birds are well represented, with species ranging from Hawfinch and Bullfinch to those more common on the moorlands of Wales - Stonechat, Whinchat, Ring Ouzel and Wheatear, and rarities such as the Hoopoe, the Lesser Spotted Woodpecker, the Woodcock and the Red-backed Shrike have been seen here. The wetter areas provide one of the most northerly breeding grounds of the Grasshopper Warbler, and Herons, Kingfishers and various waterfowl are occasional visitors. Grass snakes are common, as are slow-worms, and adders are found more rarely towards the hills. Amphibians are lucky in that the common provides a large area which is unpolluted by pesticides, herbicides or excess fertiliser, and most species of frogs and toads occur here, as well as newts - (especially Great Crested Newts, which are becoming rare in the country as a whole).

Amongst the mammals which are found here, as well as the common rabbits, hares, foxes, badgers, stoats and weasels etc, we have the unwelcome mink and grey squirrel, and the odd escapee red deer from Eastnor Park. It may be of interest to note that the Yellow-necked Woodmouse has strong populations here, and that there are reports of an animal which only fits the description of the Edible Dormouse!

The streams and pools have various types of fish, groups of anthills prove a very special habitat, with particular plants growing closely upon them, eg wild thyme which show as pinky-purple humps amongst the taller grasses of the flat common. Even wild orchids and wild daffodils can be found if you know where and when to look!

Grasses are tremendously varied and a walk from the Welland boundary, following the course of the stream towards the Gullet, always yields an interesting collection. Fungi also abound, with almost 100 species being recorded to date. Amongst the taller plants, gorse is the most obvious and has become a problem in recent years because it tends to smother all the smaller plants as it spreads due to lack of grazing. Of great interest is the presence of about 60 black poplars, mostly pollarded. This tree is now rare in Britain, and Castlemorton Common has probably the best collection left. They are usually found in small groups near dwellings, as they were formerly used for many purpose by the commoners. By pollarding them, ie cutting of the stem at about chest height, a whole clutch of straight branches is produced, and by having a group of them, often round a pond as at Mount Pleasant and up towards the Gullet, it was possible to leave some to grow bigger, giving poles of different sizes. The young branches were used for rough basketry, the older ones for fence poles, for splitting to use in wattle and daub walls, or for ladders etc. The biggest, from the oldest trees, produced a renewable source of fuel.

Black Poplars near Swinyard Car Park.

Black Poplar replanting near Swinyard Car Park.

Proposal for an earth bank with oak and larch forest transplants with a temporary fence, submitted by Tim Cameron, November 1972.

The Malvern Hills Conservators has recently taken steps to propagate some of these trees, to ensure their continued survival. A very fine specimen of black poplar stands on the common in front of Hollybush Church.

Probably in 1974, a row of oak and larch were planted on the common to screen parts of Mount Pleasant's agricultural buildings. A proposal a large earth bank for the same purpose was rejected.

Mount Pleasant, January 2020.

Building Styles and Materials

There are buildings on, and around, the common, which date from the 15th Century to the present, and which represent all the different architectural periods. The obvious styles, eg Georgian, can be seen, but many of them, particularly the bigger houses, are in fact a hotch-potch of improvement and addition, so that one house may have parts dating from

1450, and others from Victorian times. It is probably better to concentrate on the materials used in the buildings, and how these reflect the influence of the landscape. Malvern stone is a poor building material, very heavy, and, being igneous, has no good bedding or jointing planes - in other words it is impossible to carve, and the pieces very rarely have two faces at right angles.

Walls are usually built of two sections using any flat faces on the outside with a rubble and lime-and-marl mortar filling. Where two right-angled faces are needed, for instance on corners or around doorways and windows, bricks, timber, or some imported carvable stone had to be used. (Welland church is a very good example of this style). However, many of the old farm houses and outbuildings near the hills were built out of this clumsy material, simply because it was so near and therefore convenient, but it is noticeable that the use of the stone, very prevalent in buildings close to the hills, dies out completely in less than a mile away from them.

Lower down the common, especially in the valleys, there are some very good examples of wattle-and-daub (locally called wattle-and-dab). However, although there is no good building stone to hand there was plenty of big Chase timber, elm and oak, for the main construction of the houses, with plenty of hazel and black poplar for the wattle (basket work) infill between the main timbers, and the clay, or daub, with which to plaster the wattle panels. The timbers were painted with tar-type mixture, to keep out the wood-boring insects, and the daub was covered in a mixture or whitening and tallow, which made it waterproof, so that the clay would not be easily washed away. Add to this the use of thatch, because there was no suitable material for roof-tiles, and you have the typical black and white 'half timbered' style of architecture, which is found all across the Severn Valley as far as the Cotswolds.

In the south eastern part of the common there are a few buildings, eg the outbuildings at Biddles Farm, just south of the Robin Hood, which are made of a greyish sandstone, where a few narrow outcrops of this occur. It is sometimes called the Arden sandstone, and being a sedimentary rock, it will split into fairly good rectangular pieces.

On the hill at Coombe Green Common, above the Post Office there are many depressions, locally called the Foxholes, which are the remains of the quarries from which Iron Age man dug the Arden sandstone in order to build the strong dry-stone walls of the fort on Midsummer Hill. Many red-brick farmhouses, with white sills and surrounds to the windows, date from the Georgian period.

Since Victorian times, it has been possible to import materials from outside the area, so that now there are even some buildings which incorporate Cotswold stone! However, the houses around the common generally maintain the mixture of Malvern stone and half-timbering, a good example of vernacular styles.

Chapter 13

COOMBE GREEN COMMON

Coombe Green Common, 48.67 acres, is privately owned by Birtsmorton Court, home of Nigel Dawes, Lord of the Manor of Birtsmorton, and his family. It abuts Castlemorton Common on Golden Valley, the boundary running diagonally across the road between Summercoombe and Millpond Cottage; and between The Homestead and Little Orchards diagonally across what is known as The Cut. It follows the parish boundary, marked with a red line.

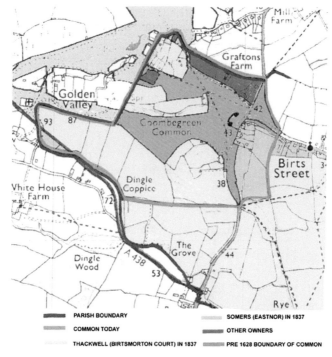

Coombe Green Common.

King Charles's map of 1628 (See Chapter 1) shows Coombe Green common as belonging to "Birch Morton Court." It portrays the common as larger than it today and was measured at 141.01 acres

The brown line indicates the probable larger extent of the common, which is just over 162 acres. It is difficult to reconcile this with the 141 acres above. Taking out the enclosures would account for 15 acres and as the southern boundary is uncertain, and taking out the Somers land to the east Gloucester Road would account for 20 acres.

Brian Smith's book "A History of Little Malvern" explains that Westminster Abbey made assarts in Castlemorton and Birtsmorton in 1241, which were enlarged four years later. [51] An assart is an area of land cleared from a Royal Forest for agriculture.

The King's Third comprised the fields between the present common, Dingle Coppice and the parish boundary just to the east of Hollybush Church.

The track that aligns with the end of Birts Street is believed to be an old drove road.

In the field immediately above The Grove there is evidence of a medieval settlement – house platforms, ridge and furrow trackways.

At the top of the common, below The Lodge Inn, there is evidence of a medieval/post mediaeval possible homestead (toft), visible as a rectilinear raised platform.

There is evidence of medieval ploughing on the common.

From The Gloucester Citizen, 16 August 1921: The 2nd Gloucester British Boy Scouts' second annual camp was held this year on Birtsmorton Common, Worcestershire, from Sunday, 30th July, to August 13th. Fifty scouts attended.

During World War II the common was used as a battle training area by the 7th Worcestershire Battalion Home Guard.

Commoners Rights

All commoners with rights to graze animals on Castlemorton Common also have rights to graze on Coombe Green Common. However, a few properties with rights to graze on Coombe Green Common only have rights to put their animals out onto Coombe Green Common. They cannot, of course, prevent their animals from straying onto Castlemorton, because it is illegal to fence common land. This is known as the right of intercommoning.

Managing the Common

The common is looked after by Friends of Coombe Green Common led by Sue Windle. Especially, they carefully maintain the feature of the old gravel pit under advice from Worcestershire Archaeological Society. They are represented on Castlemorton Commons Co-ordinating Committee by Sue Windle.

Work is undertaken by local volunteers and contractors paid for by fundraising and grants from Birtsdmorton Parish Council, principally for the clearance of bracken and thistles.

Of interest is the mature oak on the top of the Foxhills which has the plaque on it commemorating the Coronation of 1937. On the hill at Coombe Green Common above the Post Office there are many depressions, locally called the Foxholes, which are the remains of the quarries from which Iron Age man dug the Arden sandstone in order to build the strong dry-stone walls of the fort on Midsummer Hill.

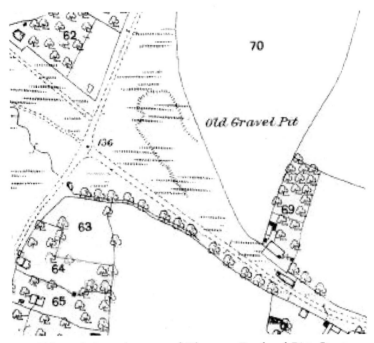

Old gravel pit on the corner of Gloucester Road and Birts Street.

The old gravel pit.

Foxholes.

Bridge over the stream.

Worcestershire Wildlife Trust produced a report on Coombe Green Common in 2007. It commended the area as highly valuable site for flora and fauna. The common is visited by glow worms, a rare thing nowadays. The common scored 18 when 13 is the threshold for grassland to be of Special Wildlife Site quality.

Mark Bowden's book, "The Malvern Hills - An Ancient Landscape", refers to them as grassed over quarries, medieval or possibly earlier.

There is a bridge over a small stream that flows across the common from a spring on Golden Valley.

The Mission Room

The Mission Room or Mission Hall has been known by various names, including the Tin Tank, The Tin Hut, The Tin Room or The Tin Tabernacle.

It stands on the south eastern corner of the junction

between Gloucester Road and Birts Street. Originally paid for by Lady Somers, it was moved from Hollybush in 1904. It has been used as a place of worship and for the Sunday School and youth club, for Parish Council Meetings and for various social activities and gatherings including whist drives, snooker, darts and coits.

The 1937 tithe map shows the plot of land as a "new enclosure", implying the land for it had been taken from the common. It belonged to Eastnor Estate until 1942, when it was sold to Worcester Diocesan Board of Finance. In about 2000 it was purchased by Mr & Mrs Neil Greenhalf as an artist's studio for their son, but planning permission was refused due to lack of car parking space. In 2019 planning permission was conversion to a dwelling was also refused, so it sits there apparently with no future.

Its full history has been researched by Jenny Fryman and was published in Volume 2 of the Birtsmorton Castlemorton and Hollybush Archive Journal, 2019.

The Mission Room.

Chapter 14

MARSH GREEN COMMON

Marsh Green Common (also known as Lower Common), comprises 34 ½ acres. In 1964 it was offered to Castlemorton Parish Council by the owners, the Church Commissioners, for £20. This was by way of 'compensation' for the Parish Council not being able to purchase Castlemorton Common. However, the Parish Council did not take up this offer and it was sold to Bryan Smith of Hillend Court on 16 June 1965. On 26 July 2005 it was transferred into the joint names of Bryan Smith, his wife Margaret and their daughter Alison Brittain. Following the deaths Bryan and Margaret Smith, it is currently owned by the Trustees of the Estate of the late Margaret Smith, and Alison Brittain.

Its unusual shape requires some explanation and it may be that it served as link between Castlemorton and the Tewkesbury Road, a sort of drove road for taking animals to market. A track is marked to the sharp bend past Castlemorton Church near Ruells Farm, and a footpath also links the western end of it to Heron Lane, the bridleway by the Severn Trent Works next to Castlemorton School. The tithe map of 1839 shows it as belonging to the Dean and Chapter of Westminster, but 'occupied' by the Freeholders of Castlemorton. No tithe rent was paid.

The fields embraced by the curve of common belonged mainly (in 1839) to Thomas Rawson and William Lane. The northern fields were known as Thorney Common Meadow and were divided into small strips and rented out to individuals. The fields in the 'v' towards the south of the common were similarly divided and known as Banfield, part of the Banfield Enclosure.

The meadows were enclosed in 1845, together with Wetfield Meadow (which had also been divided into small strips) to the east of the southern end of the common, in Birtsmorton.

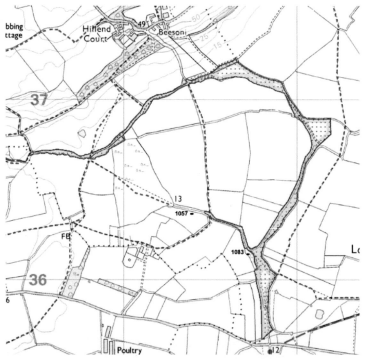

Marsh Green Common. The map is taken from Magic Maps and some of the area has not been shaded in green, but only dotted in green. However, it is all common land. (Magic Maps)

Commoners Rights

Originally there were 13 registered owners of Commoners Rights, but in 1970 Bryan Smith of Hillend Court disputed

7 of them. In 1974, none of these 7 claimants appeared at the hearing, so their claims were voided. Those with rights today are: New House Farm, Marsh End Farm, Hillend Court, Upper Green Farm, Worcestershire County Council and Gunnells.

Houses

The 1839 Tithe Map shows three houses adjacent to the common.

House No 1083, was owned by The Dean & Chapter of Westminster and was rented to Joseph Bannister (Banaster). It comprised a cottage with outbuildings, a garden and included field No 1118 below it.

In 1841, he was living there with his wife (aged 70) and still working as an Agricultural Labourer.

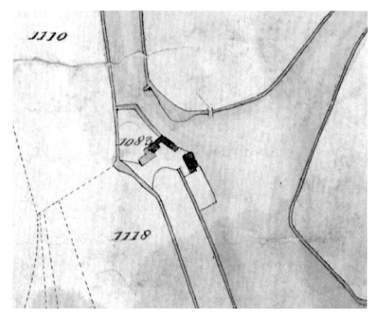

No 1083.

It is not obvious in the 1851 Census, but in 1861 was occupied by Mary Tainton, aged 85, a pauper. In 1891 it was occupied by Thomas Panting, aged 24, a Labourer; his wife Charlotte (Glover), their 2 year old son, and Matilda Sheen (sister in law).

By 1901 it had gone out of use. One local farmer remembers seeing the foundations many years ago, in exceptionally dry weather, but there is nothing to see today.

No 1057, owned by John Sturkey and rented to Richard Niblett. It was known as Summer Cottage or Summer Leasow (leasow means pasture) and from 1841 to 1891 was rented to the Webb family. The last occupants were Elizabeth Webb, aged 45, Market Woman, her two sisters and her two brothers. No trace of it remains today.

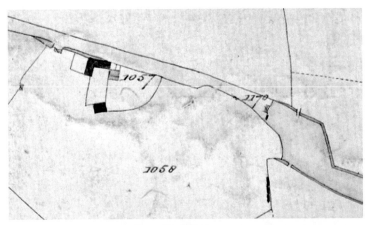

No 1057.

Forest Cottage (No 833). In 1839, owned by the Thomas Rawson (who owned a great deal of surrounding land) and occupied by Thomas Gale – cottage and garden.

In 1841, occupied by Thomas Gale, Agricultural Labourer (aged 40), his wife Mary (aged 35), their children Mary (aged 13), Thomas (aged 10), Ann (aged 6), William (aged 5) and George (aged 1).

In 1851, occupied by Thomas Gale, Agricultural Labourer (aged 56), his wife Mary (aged 47), their children William, Agricultural Labourer (aged 16), George, Agricultural Labourer (aged 10), (aged 17) and a lodger, George King, Agricultural Labourer (aged 13).

In 1861, occupied by William Gale (Agricultural Labourer (aged 24), wife Eliza, Gloveress (aged 24) and their son Thomas W (aged 3).

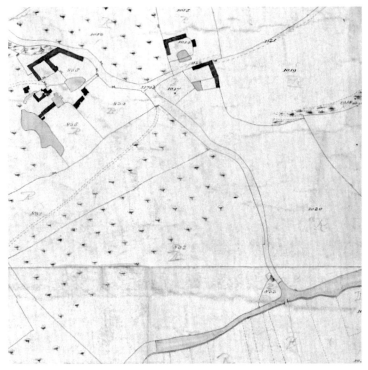

Forest Cottage is in the south east corner.

In 1871, William Gale (Agricultural Labourer (aged 34), wife Eliza, Gloveress (aged 34) and their son Thomas W (aged 3).

In 1881, William Gale (Farm Labourer (aged 44), wife Eliza, Gloveress (aged 44) and their children Thomas, Labourer, (aged 13), Mary (aged 7) and Ellen (aged 8m).

In 1891, occupied by Thomas Panting, Farmer (aged 62) and his wife Harriet (aged 59).

In 1901, identified as Forest Cottage, occupied by James Pingree, General Agricultural Labourer (aged 33) and his sister Harriet (aged 44).

In 1911, occupied by James Pingree, Farm Labourer (aged 63), his niece Annie Ellen Moore (aged 34), nephew Henry Henry Herbert Ellen, Estate Agents Clerk (aged 28) and niece Ethel Maude Ellen (aged 24).

The southern end of the common.

NOTES

1) Thomas Higgins, John Hill, John Rayer, W Lane, James Hart, George Westons, John Price, John Lane, Thomas Tombs, George Kings, W Dee, John Smith, George Lanes, W Clintons, James Copner, John Tanner, William Pinson junior and William Price.

2) The case revolved around an ejectment in June 1835, for a small encroachment containing about 12 perches, made by one Edward Jakeman about 25 years since. This may refer to Edward Jakeman's House, to the north east of Hollybed Common. This encroachment adjoined the encroachment alleged to have been made by Edward Arnold in 1767 (the premises in question in this case). Although judgment had been recovered for Jakeman's encroachment, the Dean and Chapter had not actually taken possession, and Sarah Clarke, the tenant, still remained the occupier of the whole. The ejectment was brought to recover Jakeman's encroachment as well as Arnold's. The defending solicitors accused the Dean and Chapter of trying to fix them with the costs of both actions, when one had already been settled (but not enforced). They wrote "We have had sufficient experience of the proceedings and liberality of the Dean and Chapter to satisfy us that they are determined to give up nothing which is not wrested from them by force. It was manifest to every person in court that the case of the Dean and as regards part of the cottage standing upon the waste, was breaking down under the cross-examination their own witnesses: one of them stated that half the house stood upon the waste, another that part of the kitchen only; another that the chimney; and another would not venture swear that any part of the cottage stood more than a yard from the centre of the hedge. We had, moreover, a complete answer to this part of the case: we had witnesses, the men who dug out the foundations for the cottage, the workmen employed in erecting it, and the person for whom it was built, who gave scrupulous directions that no part should be placed upon the waste; besides a great body of other evidence".

3) A tithe, or a tenth part of income, was originally to pay for the parish priest. The Tithe Commutation Act of 1836 replaced tithes with an annual rent charge - based on the assumption that a certain number of bushels of corn were worth £100.

4) Sometimes shown as D & C of W on old maps.

5) Buddenhill, Micklefield and Welland Meadow, Witbury, Wallredding, Bafield and Wetfield Meadow.

6) Commons at Welland, Hanley Castle and Upton had already been enclosed and the land shared out.

7) Signed by J A Higgins, John Rayer Lane, James Hart, Michael Thurold (for Earl Somers), Edwin Meacham.

8) In 1872 there is a newspaper account of horse races formerly having taken place on Castlemorton Common.

9) This has been dated to 1906 as Cazalet said he had been living in Castlemorton for 19 years and he bought The Bannut Tree in 1887, but may refer to the enquiry.

10) First elected in 1894 under the Local Government Act of that year.

11) By renting land, principally from Lady Somers of Eastnor. The main area was the portion of the King's Third adjacent to Broomy Hill Coppice. See map in Chapter 1.

12) An Act for the better regulation of commons and open spaces.

13) Draft by-laws presented to the Parish Council for discussion and were largely accepted without change. They were based on those bye-laws already on those parts of the Malvern Hills owned by Malvern Hills Conservators.

The Bye-laws approved by the Minister of Health 22 June 1928 are shown below:

1. *Throughout these Bye-Laws the expression of the "Council" means the Rural District Council of Upton on Severn in the County of Worcester and the expression "The Common" means the piece of land with the ponds, streams, paths and roads, thereon commonly known as Castlemorton Common,*

Hollybed Common, Shadybank Common and Marsh Green or Lower Common, situate in the Parish of Castlemorton, in the County of Worcester, and referred to as "The Common" in the scheme approved under the Commons Act, on the 23rd day of August 1927, by the Ministry of Agriculture and Fisheries.

2. *A person shall not without lawful authority deposit on the Common or any part thereof or in any pond or stream thereon any road sand, materials for repair of roads, or any rubbish, litter, wood, or other matter.*

3. *A person shall not without lawful authority dig, cut, or take any turf sods, gravel, sand, clay or substance on or from the common; or without lawful authority cut, fell or otherwise carelessly, or negligently injure any gorse, heather, timber or any other tree, shrub, brushwood or other plant growing thereon.*

4. *A person who in exercise of any right of Common or other right over the Common shall dig or take turf, sods, sand, gravel, clay or other substance, or cut, fell or take trees or underwood on or from the Common shall not commit any unnecessary damage to the Common or the turf, trees, shrub, brushwood, gorse, heather, fern, grass or other natural products thereon.*

   He shall not dig or take turf, sods, sand, gravel or clay or other substance or cut, fell or take trees or underwood on or from any part of the Common which is temporarily enclosed by the Council for the revival of the turf, shrubs, trees, underwood, plants or grasses thereon, or set apart for games, if similar turf or other respective substances can conveniently be dug, or taken or cut or felled from some other part of the Common.

5. *A person shall not carelessly or negligently deface any part of any fence, seat, shelter, pavilion, notice board or any other thing put up or maintained by the Council on the Common.*

6. *A person shall not wilfully or improperly remove any fence, fixed seat, shelter, pavilion, notice board or any other thing put up or maintained by the Council on the Common.*

7. *A person shall not without lawful authority post or paint any*

bill, placard, advertisement or any notice on any tree, fence, erection or notice-board on the Common.

8. *A person shall not on the Common without lawful authority catch any bird or set any trap, or net, or lay any snare for birds, or any other animals, or take any bird's eggs or nests, or shoot, or chase any game, or other animal on the Common.*

9. *A person shall not without lawful authority draw upon the Common any carriage, cart, caravan, truck, motor vehicle, motor cycle or other vehicle, or without the consent of the Council, or other lawful authority, erect or permit to remain on the Common any building, shed, tent, fence, post, rail or other structure, whether used in connection with the playing of games or not. Provided that this Bye-law shall not be deemed to apply to any offence which is punishable under 193 of the Law of Property Act, 1925.*

    It shall be lawful for any Officer of the Council to remove from the Common any structure erected thereon in contravention with this Byelaw.

10. *A person shall not without lawful authority (except in the case of a Fair lawfully held), place on the Common any photographic cart, or any show, exhibition, swing, roundabout, or any other like thing, and any Officer of the Council may, after due warning, lawfully remove from the Common anything placed upon the Common in contravention of this Byelaw.*

11. *A person shall not without any lawful authority light any fire upon the Common. Provided that this Bye-law shall not be deemed to apply to any offence which is punishable under 193 of the Law of Property Act, 1925.*

12. *A person shall not without any lawful authority fire or discharge any firearm, or to the danger or damage of any person throw or discharge any stone or other missile upon the Common.*

13. *A Groom or other person shall not without lawful authority exercise, train or break in any horse on the Common.*

14. *A person shall not without any lawful authority land on or*

depart from the Common in an aeroplane, or other flying machine except in the case of accident or other sufficient cause.

15. *A person shall not without any lawful authority turn out or permit to remain on the Common any cattle, sheep, or other animals. It shall be lawful, after due warning, for any Officer of the Council to remove from the Common any cattle, sheep or other animal being upon the common in contravention of this Byelaw.*

16. *A person shall not in any part of the Common wilfully obstruct, disturb, interrupt or annoy any other person in the proper use of the Common.*

17. *A person shall not hinder of obstruct any Officer in the exercise of his powers or duties under the scheme dated the 23rd day of August, 1927, or of any of the foregoing Byelaws made thereunder.*

18. *Any person who shall offend against any of the foregoing Byelaws shall be liable for every such offence to a penalty of £2.*

    Provided nevertheless that the Court of Summary Jurisdiction before whom any such proceedings may be taken in respect of any such offence may, if the Court think fit, adjudge the payment of any less sum of the full amount imposed by the Byelaw.

19. *Any Officer of the Council may after due warning remove or exclude from the Common any person who within his view commits or whom reasonably suspects of committing an offence against any of the foregoing Byelaws or against the Vagrancy Act, 1824.*

20. *Nothing in the foregoing Byelaws shall prejudice or affect any right of the person or persons entitled as Lord or Lords of the Manor or Manors or otherwise to the soil of the Common, or any part thereof, or any persons claiming under him of them which is lawfully exercisable in, over, under, or on the soil or surface of the Common in connection with game, or with mines, minerals or other sub-strata or otherwise, or prejudice or affect*

any right of the Commoners in or over the Common or the
lawful use of any highway or thoroughfare on the Common or
affect any power of obligation to repair any such highway or
thoroughfare.

14) John William Wilson, PC, JP (22 October 1858 – 18 June 1932) was a British chemical manufacturer and politician who served for 27 years as a member of parliament. He lived at Perrycroft on Jubilee Drive, Malvern. The house was designed by Charles Voysey and the gardens are opened to the public.

15) Foxhall lies half way up the track to Pink Cottage and was owned by the National Trust until 2005.

16) It has not been possible to identify her house.

17) Reasons for Notification:

Castlemorton Common is situated at the foot off the Malvern Hills. It lies on soils derived from drift deposits which overlie the impermeable Keuper marl and consists mainly of low lying rough pasture with marshy areas, streams and frequent patches of scrub. The prime importance of the site is its grassland communities. These include areas of dry neutral unimproved grassland which are relatively species rich. They are dominated by a mixture of grasses, such as crested dog's-tail Cynosurus cristatus, red fescue Festuca rubra and mat-grass Nardus stricta. The soils over most of the area are slightly acidic as indicated by the presence of sorrel Rumex acetosa and tormentil Potentilla erecta, but in a few places species preferring more base-rich conditions are evident such as mouse-ear hawkweed Hieracium pilosella and stemless thistle Cirsium acaule. Small areas of semi-improved grassland occur alongside the road. In the grassland there are many active ant hills, especially in the drier areas. These provide a valuable food source for the green woodpecker Picus viridis. In some areas the water table is very high and this has given rise to a wet grassland community characterised by tufted hair-grass Deschampsia cespitosa. Two streams flow through the site bordered by marshy grassland, having an abundance of rushes including soft rush Juncus effusus, hard rush J. inflexus, conglomerate rush

J. conglomeratus and jointed rush J. articulatus. These areas are particularly species rich and include several uncommon species such as marsh arrowgrass Triglochin palustris, flatsedge Blysmus compressus, fleabane Pulicaria dysenterica, common spotted orchid Dachtylorhiza fuchsii, tubular water-dropwort Oenanthe fistulosa, parsley water-dropwort O. lachenalii and the rare narrow-leaved water-dropwort O. silaifolia. The marshy grassland is a favoured habitat for birds such as snipe Gallinago gallinago and reed bunting Emberiza schoeniclus. In the north east corner of the site is a small pond which in summer becomes completely overgrown with floating sweet-grass Glyceria fluitans, creeping bent Agrostis stolonifera and marsh foxtail Alopecurus geniculatus. Lesser marshwort Apium inundatum, an uncommon species, has been recorded from here. Scattered over the site are areas of scrub consisting of gorse Ulex europaeus, western gorse U. gallii, hawthorn Crataegus monogyna, bramble Rubus fruticosus agg. and rose Rosa spp. The scrub is valuable for insects and provides nesting sites for birds such as the stonechat Saxicola torquata. At the north eastern end of the site is a small area of broad-leaved woodland containing several pollards of the native black poplar Populus nigra – a species with a very restricted distribution in Britain.

18)   There is a site of an alleged castle by Castlemorton Church on "The Tump". There has been no archaeological investigation and it is believed a castle may have been here because it looks similar to other sites known to have had castles.

19)   There are the rights of commoners to graze animals (Right of Pasture), graze pigs on fallen acorns and beech seed woodlands (Right of Pannage) take fallen wood and loppings for burning or construction; and gorse and furze (Right of Estovers), fish in ponds and streams (Right of Piscary), dig peat or turf for fuel (Right of Turbary) and the right to take sand, stone, gravel or minerals for us on the Commoner's holding (Right of Common in the Soil).

20)   The common lands of England Wales are in general of immemorial antiquity. (Royal Commission on Public Land

1955-58). Probably their origin goes as far back as the Celts – before the Roman Invasion – before the birth of Christ.

By tribal custom, a 4-year crop rotation was practised. This meant growing three different crops rotation and the fourth field laying fallow. Once the crop had been harvested, the land was thrown open to grazing. Ownership of land, and possibly animals, belonged to the tribe.

During the Anglo Saxon period – from the departure of the Romans in 410 to 1066, agricultural practices changed. The method of cultivation was that of the common or open field system. The fertile land of each community was divided up into two or three open fields. These in turn were divided into strips, each of about an acre, and these strips were individuals or peasant families. However, one of the fields would lie fallow each year and all the members of the community were entitled to allow their cattle to pasture on it. In the fallow year. It became a "common field" and the members of the community had common rights of grazing over it. Land unsuitable for cultivation was known as the waste.

When the population of England and Wales was small, there was abundant land for all and common rights had no need for definition. By the 1200s the population had grown and there was a need to put some limits on common rights: who had them and their extent. This was done by proportioning rights to the size of farms – referred to as Stints or Couchant and Levant. Couchant and Levant means that the farmer could graze in the summer on common land as many beasts as he could take care of on his own land in the winter. Most common land had come into the ownership of Manorial Lords, although the peasants retained their rights to use the surface of the land. The Lord of the Manor had his own land which he farmed himself, called the Demesne Land, and other land which was common land or waste land.

There were different classes of common rights:

Freeholders had a right Appendant to their freeholds to pasture on the waste all commonable beasts (cows and sheep) that could be wintered on their own land.

Freeholders might also have Appurtenant rights, to put

goats and pigs on the waste.These were granted by the Lord of the Manor.

Rights "In Gross".These were rights that did not attach to the ownership of any particular piece of land. They were granted by the Lord to non land owners and were passed on to their heirs.These people were the biggest users of the waste.They are also called Incorporeal Hereditaments.

Right of common by reason of vicinage.These arise where two commons adjoin each other and beasts can stray from one common to the other. If you have rights to one common, then you also have rights to the other. However, your beast must start on the common to which you have rights, you cannot put them directly onto the other common. This is also known as intercommoning and Castlemorton Common intercommons with Coombe Green Common.

Between Domesday (1086) and the Black Death (1348) the population of England and Wales had trebled to just under 4 million. There was a shortage of farming land in many parts of England and marginal land, especially heaths and moors, was brought into cultivation.Thousands of farms were erected under licence from the Lord of the Manor.A survey of land use in 1688 showed that a quarter of England and Wales was waste land, used only for rough grazing.The everyday management of the land was done by the local villagers.

21) The sale particulars of what is probably Rough Chase, in 1812, stated that the purchaser was entitled to grazing rights on upwards of 1500 acres of land.

22) Prerequisites
  1. The holding must contain at least ½ acre of genuine grazing.
  2. The holding must adjoin the Common or a road bounding the Common or possess rights of green lane access to the Common.

Then
(a) Holding ½ acre to 15 acres
  Entitlement 7 sheep per acre
  Acreage of holdings in this category – 325.Total 2254

(b) Holdings 15 to 25 acres
Entitlement 5 sheep per acre
Acreage of holdings in this category – 160. Total 800

(c) Holdings over 25 acres
Entitlement 3 sheep per acre
Acreage of holdings in this category – 590. Total 1741

Grand Total 4795 sheep.

Stocking formula equivalent 5 sheep = one cow, horse, pony, goat or donkey.
It was decided that poultry would not be counted.
The discrepancy in the figures can be explained by the fact that certain applicants had applied for less rights than they were entitled to under this formula. They have accordingly been allocated the smaller figure.

23) A letter dated 11 November 1976 from the County Council Secretary and Solicitor, Mr J W Renney, set out a scheme of apportionment, acceptable to "all or the majority of claimants" agreed between the County Council and Castlemorton Commoners Association. Commoners were advised to consider their own position and notify either the Solicitor to the Commoners Association or the County Council of their acceptance or rejection and their reasons for so doing, not later than 30th November 1976. There were small number of disputes and one case was settled as late as 1977.

24) The formula produces a total number of sheep which could be grazed on the Common at any one time of 4795. The Commissioner decided that the Common could support 3132 sheep or equivalent based on the formula of four sheep per acre. The Castlemorton Commoners Association and the County Council felt that the Commissioner's figure of 3132 was unrealistic in that the commoners possessing rights would not choose to exercise them simultaneously and agreed that the Commissioner be requested to accept the figure of 4795 to compromise the dispute.

25) Ron had the rights to graze 600 sheep, although he usually put out young cattle.

26) Up to 1926, the public had no right of free access to common land. Sections 193 and 194 of the Law Property Act, which came into force on 1 January 1926, gave the public the right of access to common land or manorial waste for "air and exercise".

27) The Patch or Collins's Patch - just off New Road, bought from Montague Jakeman who grew vegetables there, Mill Pond Orchard – also known as Morgan's Orchard, Ledyatts, a small pond isolated on the common and a parcel of land both belonging to Berrow Down - four acres near Roseville Farm, ¼ acre on the south of New Road to the east of Mount Pleasant and fields adjoining the Common south of the track from Gate Cottage to Underhills Farm.

    The Conservators have also approached the other owners of two other pieces of land bounded by the common and sought to purchase it (without success). The site of an old house on Sunny Bank known as Sunnyside; and a small fenced wooded area opposite Cider Mill Cottage on the south side of Hancocks Lane known as Tippers Patch.

28) The 1884 Malvern Hills Act refers to an order of the Court of Star Chamber 5th September 1632 in which 2/3rds of the King's Chase (this includes Castlemorton Common) "should be from thenceforth and for ever for the freeholders and tenants and commoners to take their common of pasture and common of estovers therein as theretofore they had been accustomed".

29) From Hangmans Hill to the Gullet, with the Shire Ditch as the western boundary. 114 acres.

30) A precept is a levy, part of Council Tax, determined by the number of households in the parish and their level of occupancy.

31) The town of Malvern and the parishes of Colwall, Guarlford, Malvern Wells, Mathon and West Malvern.

32) At a meeting of Powick Common Committee of Malvern Hills Conservators on 22 March 1965, the Conservators proposed that the precept should be extended over their newly acquired land in Upton Rural District Council. Whilst

the Parishes would make some contribution, the bulk of the money would have to come from the County Council and Upton Rural District Council. Regarding representation, the County Council already had two representatives but if Upton contributed their number could be increased to two.

A meeting of Upton Rural District Council on 22 September 1965 recorded that Castlemorton Parish Council had objected to idea of any levy on their rate for the Conservators. The Conservators had said they wished to spend £1600 on the common over the next two years.

An undated Memorandum issued by the Conservators claimed "The Conservators have the power to extend their precept to the parishes in which their land lies, but the parishes of Castlemorton and Powick would not be able to provide the funds required".

On 2 August 1965, a working party was convened of Upton Rural District Council, Castlemorton Parish Council and the Conservators to discuss Finances and Byelaws, but there is no record of any minutes of the meeting in Worcestershire Archives.

On 8 April 1965, the Clerk to Worcestershire County Council, Mr W R Scurfield, wrote to Mr E Whatley, Clerk to the Conservators with his suggestions:

1. The Conservators should first reach a decision on Powick.
2. The Conservators should then obtain power to levy a rate in respect of all Parishes within the Upton upon Severn Rural District within which they now own land (Guarlford, Little Malvern, Castlemorton, Birtsmorton, Berrow and Powick)
3. The Conservators then work out whether the precept they now levy, extended to the extra Parishes, will give them enough money to do what they need to do.
4. If Upton Rural District Council think the extra levy has an unreasonable effect on their Parishes, they should seek help from the County Council.
5. The County Council will then be faced with requests from both the Conservators and Upton Rural District Council and will most likely agree to these.

33) Castlemorton and Welland, so far as Castlemorton Common is concerned, but apparently also Powick.

34) In 1978 a Parish Council minute records that Worcestershire County Council might pull out of paying towards the Conservators and a rate might be made on Castlemorton instead. The Parish Council again recorded its objection.

35) Objects of Castlemorton Common Association:

> To safeguard the future and identity of the Common as a working common.
>
> To support the "Commoners' in exercising their legal rights, where these have been registered and established.
>
> To keep a fair balance between the justifiable interests of the Commoners and such feasible leisure pursuits as may to-exist with these interests.
>
> To encourage social opportunities for people in the association by meetings and other gatherings.
>
> To seek constructive co-operation with the Malvern Hills Conservators for the mutual benefit of both parties.

The Committee will consist of nine members, five of them having commoners rights, but not all nine places need necessarily be filled The original committee were all local commoners, their names are well represented in the history of the area, and they are still respected as names which keep the area well rooted in the spirit of the common, so that the knowledge of the area is passed on.

Original Committee:

A Baldwin	Hay Cottage
R Bunn	Hunters Hall
M Jakeman	The Cottage
R Lloyd	Morton Green Farm
F Mears	The Joyfields
D Preece	Fair Oaks Farm
H Weaver	Mount Pleasant

36) Written by Med Snookes, who led the Association for 40 years,

standing down in 2018 due to ill health. Regular meetings are no longer held with the Conservators, liaison now being provided by the 4C's.

37) The Shindig was not held in 2018-2020, but was successfully restarted in 2021.

38) Today we also see Herdwicks and Jacobs grazing on the common.

39) The figures as hard to compare as "the hills" can mean just the hills, or the common and the hills. In 2020, about 560 sheep and 45 cattle were grazing on just the hills.

40) Purposes of Castlemorton Commons Co-ordinating Committee (4Cs):

To support the agricultural systems associated with Commoning and the management of the Commons.

To promote the conservation of the physical and natural environment of the Commons by supporting their pastoral use.

To enable Commoners, the managers of the Commons and other Stakeholders to work together to enhance the public benefits of Commoning and the Commons.

To provide a forum for discussion and input into decision making about the management and use of the Commons and Commoning

To receive relevant financial and other reports relating to the management of the Commons.

To work with stakeholders to ensure integrated outcomes for the Commons and Commoners and other users.

To provide input into the development of major projects such as existing agri-environment and future land management schemes and to assist in the delivery and management of such schemes.

To ensure that relevant environmental, landscape, cultural, recreational, heritage, legal, financial and Commoning considerations are incorporated into the ongoing management of the Commons including their use as Working Commons.

The Committee shall comprise:

3 elected active commoners.

2 people appointed by Malvern Hills Trust

1 person appointed by Mr Nigel Dawes (to represent Coombe Green Common)

2 people appointed by Castlemorton Common Association

2 people appointed by Castlemorton Parish Council

1 person appointed by Birtsmorton Parish Council

1 person appointed by Welland Parish Council

1 member elected to represent recreational interests.

41) The AONB is a partnership between DEFRA and local authorities. It is an advisory body, without any legal powers.

42) The Parish Council and local households (the 5 closest dwellings plus Eastnor Estate) were written to on 18 December 2002, with no objections forthcoming.

43) With the grant of a legal easement, prescriptive rights did not to be asserted.

44) The ability of householders to acquire prescriptive rights of access across common land generally has been a source of legal controversy. In 1993 the Court of Appeal (Hanning v Top Deck Travel [1993] 68 P&CR 14) held that prescriptive rights of vehicular access over common land could not be acquired because it was a criminal offence to drive on common land – you couldn't obtain legal rights by doing something illegal. This opened the way for profiteering freehold owners of common land and village greens to impose exorbitant charges on householders for the grant of access rights which had been used for many years. Regulations made under the Countryside and Rights of Way Act 2000 limited the amount that could be charged to scale fees of up to 2 per cent of the value of the premises; less than the 30 per cent that some common owners reportedly demanded but still a potentially material sum. As a charity, the Conservators were obliged to charge what the law then allowed. In 2004 the House of Lords (Brandwood and others v Bakewell Management Ltd. [2004] UKHL 14) overruled the Court of Appeal, holding that prescriptive rights

could be acquired where it was possible for the owner of the common to grant lawful authority to drive over the common. This puts in doubt the legality of some of the charges imposed on householders under the previous, mistaken, understanding of the law (See for example Matthews and others v Herefordshire Council, heard before HHJ Worster in the Birmingham County Court in 2011, involving Bringsty Common).

45) Jeffrey J Hart born 1942, one of 5 children of Walter Robert Hart and Mary Winfred Ridley.

46) In 1957, solicitors Smiths Gore & Co of Craven Arms wrote to Castlemorton Parish Council to say they had found that the Church Commissioners had purchased the pond by conveyance on 5 October 1877 and that it did not form part of the common. They invited interest in local residents forming an Angling Society whereby they could be let the rights to fish there and prevent people from industrial towns from fishing there. In 1959, Ledbury & District Angling Association enquired about taking on the fishing rights. In return, they would repair the dam and the banks.

47) The Parish Council asked for five conditions:

1. To retain fishing rights for parishioners without charge.
2. That it be cleared out.
3. The lease to be for 21 years only.
4. That the land was freehold and should not be registered as common land.
5. No additional rate should ever be imposed on the parish, in view of the Conservators charging for parking on the common and also for charging fishing rights for persons outside the parish.

In 1968, there was correspondence over cancelling the registration of the Millpond as Common Land. It must have been registered as common land by Upton Rural District Council and the Conservators, who now faced an objection to this by Castlemorton Parish Council. The County Council took the view that the Millpond had never ceased to be part of the common land that surrounded it and therefore the registrations should stand. In 2018, Fiona Morgan of Legal Services at Worcestershire County Council has confirmed that it is shown as common land on their definitive map and that the red ring on the map around the pond is not intended to show that it is not common land.

48) Events in 1887 were reported in the Worcestershire Chronicle, 13th August: "The 1st Worcestershire Artillery Volunteers, who have had a week's very pleasant and successful encampment at Castlemorton, were inspected last Friday by Colonel Tyler (Welsh Division Royal Artillery) in the presence of the Lord-Lieutenant of the County (Earl Beauchamp). The inspection took place on the common near the encampment, and was witnessed by a large number of people. The weather was fine, but the intense heat was found extremely oppressive. Lieutenant-Colonel C R Lyne was in command. The total number parade including officers, non-commissioned officers and band was 729. The Lord Lieutenant on his arrival was received near Welland Church by a guard of honour under the command of Lieutenant Goss. His lordship was attended by a staff consisting of Lieutenant Colonel Milwair, Major Webb, and G Somerset. Lieutenant Harcourt acted as orderly officer to Colonel Tyler. The regiment received the Lord Lieutenant in open order with the "presentation", formed quarter columns on right companies of battalions; moved to the right in fours, wheeled to the left, and advanced on the saluting base, advanced in column by half battalions, and formed quarter column on the leading companies, and marched past in lines of quarter columns; wheeled on the original base, and deployed to the left by half battalions went through the manual and firing exercises; formed quarter column on the right companies, closed to six interval between battalions, changed front half right and half left, and advanced in review order. The whole of the movements were admirably performed. The Lord-Lieutenant, addressing Lieutenant Colonel Lyne, the officers, non-commissioned officers, and men, said : I desire first of all to congratulate you your appearance here to-day in such large numbers as I think reflect credit on your regiment, collected as you are from various parts not only of this but of the adjacent

counties. I should like to express the satisfaction which it gave me as Lord-Lieutenant, yesterday, to observe your soldier-like bearing, which I think will be memorable not only the history of this county but in the history of the auxiliary forces of this country. As His Royal Highness the Duke of Cambridge expressed great satisfaction with your soldierly appearance and good behaviour, and you will hear from the proper military authorities the satisfaction felt at your behaviour, and that of all those assembled yesterday, it is not necessary for me to say anything on that point; but you will allow me perhaps, to say this, that the review could not have been brought about without great deal of organisation; without great deal of good will; without great deal of care; and without a great deal of zeal and energy on the part of those who were concerned, and I think it reflects the highest credit on those responsible for the organisation of the review that it was brought to satisfactory a conclusion The only drawback of our meeting here to-day is the extreme heat of the sun, which has somewhat curtailed your manoeuvres; but from the excellence and steadiness of the manoeuvres I have seen, I have every reason believe this regiment will continue to bear the high character it has already gained, and I glad to have had this opportunity inspecting it and of addressing it, and expressing my satisfaction at your appearance and demeanour. The regiment then marched back to the camp, where they were addressed by Colonel Tyler, who first presented a medal for 18 years good conduct to Sergeant-Major Hunter, instructor the Risca battery. In doing so he remarked that Hunter had served with exemplary conduct for 18 years, and the medal was the most worthy medal and the most worthy reward any man could receive. He was very pleased to give it to him in the presence of the whole corps. Addressing the regiment, Colonel Tyler said this was his first year as inspecting officer, and he was very to see they had turned out strong and so well after the hard work they had undergone. He knew from personal experience that nothing was so trying to men turning out day after day in the heat the sun, and the Duke of Cambridge, who was so much pleased with the regiment on the previous day, would be still more pleased with the knowledge that they had again that day turned out as well and as strong as before. He should have great pleasure in making satisfactory report of the regiment to the officer commanding the district. Lieutenant-Colonel Lyne also addressed the regiment. He said that as regarded their efficiency it would be together out of place for him to say how they had succeeded, but they had heard Colonel Tyler's remarks, they were doubtless very gratified. As regarded their conduct and discipline he was pleased to be able to say what he was going to do. There was doubt that at the end of the last training he was not satisfied - far from it - and he did not hesitate to tell them so. But he had no hesitation now in saying that, although the discipline of the corps at the last training was worse than it had ever been under his command, the discipline during the present encampment had been equal any previous occasion. The men had not only obeyed their orders but obeyed them readily. He did not wish to name batteries, but inasmuch as be singled out at the last camp two batteries for reprimand without naming them, he considered it necessary to say that they had entirely retrieved their character. He did not mean to say they were better now than any others, but he had no hesitation saying that although at the last encampment they were the worst in camp, on the present occasion they were equal to any. His thanks were due to the whole of the officers and non-commissioned officers. There were two officers he desired to single out; and the first was their adjutant. An adjutant joining Volunteer Corps laboured under great disadvantages at the first encampment, as he did not know their ways but Captain Galton had not only carried out all his work with the strictest discipline and order, but had endeared himself to every non-commissioned officer and man. (Applause) The other officer he wished to name was their most excellent Quartermaster. He did not believe any regular regiment in the Army had a better Quartermaster than Quartermaster Williams. (Applause) Their comfort depended mainly upon the Quartermaster, and his thanks and their thanks were due to him. (Applause) He had told Quartermaster Williams so in private, and he was glad to say so in the presence of the regiment. Lieutenant-Colonel

Lyne added that it had been determined by majority of the officers that it would be desirable not to go to Castlemorton for next year's encampment, but to some other part of the division. A large party of ladies and gentlemen were afterwards entertained luncheon by Lieutenant-Colonel Lyne and the officers of the regiment.

The health of the men during the encampment has been very good. There has been only one serious case of illness, and the man in question was ill when he went into camp. The repository gun competition, which usually takes place during the annual training, has this year been to a later period. It is expected that next year the encampment will be in the neighbourhood of Newport (Monmouthshire), where there are two batteries of the regiment."

49) "The Worcester Artillery as a body have encamped for the last time at Castlemorton where for a long period they have fixed their tents in alternate years. For many reasons there is cause for regret in the changed circumstances. Many pleasant weeks have been spent there, and a great advantage has been its accessibility from the various centres of companies forming the corps. There has been opportunity for friendly visit and many in Worcester will miss the interest and hospitality of inspection day in camp. Representation having been made as to the unsafe character of the ranges and upon evidence of stray shots occasionally - for, of course, bad marksmanship is the rare exception - finding their way into unwelcome places unforeseen by the architects of the range, the authorities have ordered that in future instead of going into camp at Castlemorton in alternate years the corps shall camp every year at some sea range. The rank and file doubtless will be delighted to find their future lot cast in such fair places, and it is a happy thing that the week in which they leave tools and their own interests, to bear arms in the interest of the public should be made something like a sea-side holiday. I can quite understand their feeling that the sentiment "There's no place like home" must not be taken to apply to holiday times when the sea shore is the place of places. They, at any rate, should benefit by the change, and as for those who have only gone into camp on

inspection days, when military rations have been found quite satisfactory, and no portable filter has been required, they will still be cordially welcomed by the Major if they care to take the longer journey. It will not be surprising to bear that in future years Scarborough or Llandudno, as the case may be, is overwhelmed with Worcestershire and Warwickshire visitors in early August, attracted by the double interest of the sea-side holiday and inspection or, as some people call it, luncheon day, in camp."

50) "About 100 men (some 50 of them from Worcester) the Worcestershire Artillery Volunteers Corps have been spending the Whitsuntide holiday camp Castlemorton Common, Welland, being favoured with delightful weather. The common is an ideal camping ground, has been used as such many previous occasions, and is well suited for manoeuvres. It only lacks one thing, and that is a range for the Artillery. Originally there was one, but was closed by the War Office, being declared unsafe. It is to be hoped that the matter will be taken up by the County Council, or other authorities, and new range provided, as this is very essential part of Artillery efficiency. On Saturday last, at noon, the Kidderminster contingent, with guns, arrived at Worcester, and joined the headquarters battery, and these left the city together. On the road from Welland, the Malvern detachment joined them, and all arrived at the camping ground at four o'clock. Tents were soon pitched, tea partaken of, and at 10 o'clock all turned in for the night. Reveille sounded at 5.30 on Sunday morning, and officers and non-coms, paraded at 6.30 for sword drill. Two hours later, breakfast having been taken, the horses were hooked to the guns and marched on to the common until 11 clock. Dinner was served at 12.30, and drill again engaged in from two to four. After tea, the men were allowed to leave until 10 o'clock, and the bugle sounded lights out at 10.15. The sun was very hot, and by Sunday night many officers and men began to look quite bronzed. At 6.30 on Monday morning there was sword drill under command of Major Larkworthy, and during the morning drill on the common. At 2.30 the whole of the men, with all the guns, paraded on the common, in review

order, for mounted inspection by Colonel Bland, R.A., who was accompanied by Lieutenant Neal, ADC.

The Brigade Division was drawn up line, under Major E.W. Larkworthy, the other officers present being Captains R E Lvon (Malvern), E C Bullock (Worcester). H Smith (Kidderminster), Lieutenants and A A Maund (Worcester), Claughton (Malvern), and Taylor, and Surgeon-Lieutenant Oldham (Kidderminster). The Inspecting Officer was received with a general salute, and he at once made a thorough inspection of the men, guns, horses, etc. He then took his position at the saluting point and the brigade marched past in column of batteries at half intervals, and also ranked past in single file. The batteries then came into action, under their battery commanders, by the deliberate and direct method, on a supposed enemy advancing with artillery and infantry over the hills from the direction of Ledbury, both waggon and limber supply being used show how expeditiously a large amount of ammunition could be brought into action in a very short time, if necessary. Several different positions were taken up, and the gun detachments were carefully inspected in gunnery. The brigade afterwards formed up and advanced in review order on their original alignment. On the batteries being formed up at close interval, Colonel Bland, addressing the corps, said it was with very great pleasure that congratulated them on their smart appearance. Their appointments were clean, and their horses in excellent condition, and reflected great credit on those who had had the chief care of them. All the manoeuvres had been efficiently executed, and had proved the great advantage of the corps being able to avail itself of such opportunities as that for doing mounted drills. There were, of course, a few minor mistakes, but those could be easily rectified. The Inspecting Officer suggested that the men should wear regulation boots. He hoped to see them at gun practice in camp later on, when he would further thoroughly inspect them. The brigade afterwards marched back to camp, where they immediately loaded their stores on the baggage wagons, and started for their various drill stations at 5.30. The Worcester and Kidderminster detachments arrived at Worcester 9.30, having stopped 15 minutes for refreshments at Clevelode. Kidderminster billeted in Worcester, and left the next morning. The band of the headquarters battery (Worcester), under Bandmaster Somers, played selections during the inspection. The Corporation horses were much admired. There is some talk of the guns being painted khaki colour.

The pleasure of the camp was greatly marred a rather serious accident which befell Captain Frank Penny, Ombersley Road, Worcester. While mounted drill was proceeding on Sunday, Captain Penny had just sheathed his sword, when his horse reared and fell backwards on its rider. The horse then, in attempting to get up, rolled back on the officer a second time, and crushed some of his ribs, causing internal injuries. Captain Penny was carried into his tent and medically attended, and afterwards removed to Worcester. It is hoped that the injuries will not prove so serious as was at first expected. Captain Penny is much liked by his fellow officers and the men under his command, and much sympathy is felt with him and Mrs Penny and family.

51) This may refer to Golden Valley, but having read the text in his reference there is no specific reference to Castlemorton and Birtsmorton (only to Malvern), so I cannot confirm this. He says "William Comin renders an account – The same [renders an account] of 1 mark [13s 4d] from the farm of the market of Malvern. [This is not an agricultural farm. The term "farm" means that the Crown, in return for a lump sum, has given someone the right to receive the income from the market]. The same [renders an account] of 4 score and 8 pounds 16s [£88 16s] from assarts [newly cleared patches of land]".

BIBLIOGRAPHY AND REFERENCES

As I carried out my research, I never had in mind to publish it as book, so I did not keep a comprehensive list of sources. To the best of my recollection, a list of people who assisted, and publications I referred to, are given below. If I have missed any out, then I apologise, and of course any errors, are my own.

A History of Malvern, Brian Smith
Alison Brittain
Amanda Simons
Colin Weaver
Denise Hobbs
Dermot Weaver
Diana Sharman
Forest Law, Cora Weaver
George Demidowicz
Historic England
Jenny Fryman
John Baylis
Magic Maps
Malvern Hills Trust – Susan Satchell and Jonathan Bills
Mary Watts
Mary Weaver
Med Snookes
Roger Jakeman
Roots of England, Michael Wood
Royal Commission on Common Land 1955-56
Sandra Smallwood
Sue Windell
The Society of Antiquaries
Tim Cameron
The Forest and Chase of Malvern, Pamela Hurle
Worcestershire County Council Archives
Worcestershire Wildlife Trust
Valerie Snookes